# Zabbix Network Monitoring Essentials

Your one-stop solution to efficient network monitoring with Zabbix

**Andrea Dalle Vacche**

**Stefano Kewan Lee**

[PACKT] open source*
PUBLISHING        community experience distilled

BIRMINGHAM - MUMBAI

# Zabbix Network Monitoring Essentials

First published: February 2015

Production reference: 1210215

Published by Packt Publishing Ltd.
Livery Place
35 Livery Street
Birmingham B3 2PB, UK.

ISBN 978-1-78439-976-4

www.packtpub.com

# Credits

**Authors**
Andrea Dalle Vacche

Stefano Kewan Lee

**Reviewers**
Ravi Bhure

Nicholas Pier

Nicola Volpini

**Commissioning Editor**
Amarabha Banerjee

**Acquisition Editor**
Nikhil Karkal

**Content Development Editor**
Siddhesh Salvi

**Technical Editor**
Humera Shaikh

**Copy Editor**
Sarang Chari

**Project Coordinator**
Kranti Berde

**Proofreaders**
Simran Bhogal

Linda Morris

**Indexer**
Hemangini Bari

**Graphics**
Disha Haria

**Production Coordinator**
Aparna Bhagat

**Cover Work**
Aparna Bhagat

# About the Authors

**Andrea Dalle Vacche** is a highly skilled IT professional with over 14 years of experience in the IT industry and banking. He graduated from Università degli Studi di Ferrara with an information technology certification. This laid the technology foundation that Andrea has built on ever since. Andrea has acquired various industry-respected accreditations, which include Cisco, Oracle, RHCE, ITIL, and of course, Zabbix. Throughout his career, he has worked in many large-scale environments, often in roles that have been very complex, on a consultant basis. This has further enhanced his growing skill set, adding to his practical knowledge base and increasing his appetite for theoretical technical studying.

Andrea's love for Zabbix came from his time spent in the Oracle world as a database administrator/developer. His time was spent mainly on reducing ownership costs, specializing in monitoring and automation. This is where he came across Zabbix and the flexibility it offered, both technically and administratively. With this as a launch pad, Andrea was inspired to develop Orabbix, the first open source software to monitor Oracle's complete integration with Zabbix. He has published a number of articles on Zabbix-related software, such as DBforBIX. His projects are publicly available at `http://www.smartmarmot.com`. Currently, Andrea is working as a senior architect for a leading global investment bank in a very diverse and challenging environment. He deals with many aspects of the Unix/Linux platforms as well as many types of third-party software, which are strategically aligned to the bank's technical roadmap. In addition to this title, Andrea Dalle Vacche is a coauthor of *Mastering Zabbix*, *Packt Publishing*.

**Stefano Kewan Lee** is an IT consultant with more than 12 years of experience in system integration, security, and administration. He is a certified Zabbix specialist in large environments holds a Linux administration certification from the LPI and a GIAC GCFW certification from SANS Institute. When he's not busy breaking websites, he lives in the countryside with his two cats and two dogs and practices martial arts. In addition to this title, Stefano Kewan Lee is a coauthor of *Mastering Zabbix*, *Packt Publishing*.

# About the Reviewers

**Ravi Bhure** is basically an IT engineer with niche skills, such as Chef, Cloud Ansible, SaltStack, Python, Ruby, and Shell/Bash. He also writes code for infrastructure, daily IT operations, and so on. In short, he is fond of using his skills and knowledge of fault-tolerant solutions for the day-to-day maintenance of mission-critical production infrastructure.

Ravi started interacting with computers since 1996 when he got his first computer at home. Things changed very fast, and in 1998, he entered the magical world of the Internet ☺ for the first time ever, which changed his life! He started his own cyber cafe in 1999. In 2004, he got his first job as a field engineer, hired to maintain and support VRI UFO systems. After 2 years, he moved to Pune and worked with many organizations, such as Vyom Labs, Glam India, Symphony, and Dhingana.

The most happening and interesting fact about his diverse exposure is that he is from an arts background. Yes, he holds a bachelor's degree in arts from SRTM University, Nanded, Maharashtra, India. And we all will have to agree that he has the art to solve problems ☺, a great inspiration for people who are non engineers!

Currently, Ravi is associated with OpexSoftware as a senior DevOps engineer.

**Nicholas Pier** is a network engineer in the managed services / professional services field. His experience includes designing data center network infrastructures with virtualization and SAN solutions, web development, and writing middleware for business applications. At the time of writing this, Nicholas holds a number of industry certifications, including the Cisco CCNP, VMware VCP5-DCV, and various other Cisco and CompTIA certifications. In his free time, he indulges in his passion for craft beer, distance running, and reading.

I'd like to thank Packt Publishing for this opportunity!

**Nicola Volpini** has been playing with technology from a young age, having a hard time resisting the urge to disassemble complex toys or kitchen appliances.

The love for computers originated around his tenth birthday, when he accidentally toasted his first CPU. This episode only increased his fascination for computers, and the accidents, fortunately, stopped.

For the past 10 years, he's been working as an IT professional, specializing in enterprise networking and system administration. Experimenting with the most diverse technologies in the field and being an avid fan of the FOSS philosophy, Linux, and *BSD, he dreams of seeing the collaborative thinking of the FOSS movement help inspire the world.

He's currently working at Stockholm, Sweden, where he resides with his girlfriend.

# www.PacktPub.com

## Support files, eBooks, discount offers, and more

For support files and downloads related to your book, please visit www.PacktPub.com.

Did you know that Packt offers eBook versions of every book published, with PDF and ePub files available? You can upgrade to the eBook version at www.PacktPub. com and as a print book customer, you are entitled to a discount on the eBook copy. Get in touch with us at service@packtpub.com for more details.

At www.PacktPub.com, you can also read a collection of free technical articles, sign up for a range of free newsletters and receive exclusive discounts and offers on Packt books and eBooks.

https://www2.packtpub.com/books/subscription/packtlib

Do you need instant solutions to your IT questions? PacktLib is Packt's online digital book library. Here, you can search, access, and read Packt's entire library of books.

## Why subscribe?

- Fully searchable across every book published by Packt
- Copy and paste, print, and bookmark content
- On demand and accessible via a web browser

## Free access for Packt account holders

If you have an account with Packt at www.PacktPub.com, you can use this to access PacktLib today and view 9 entirely free books. Simply use your login credentials for immediate access.

# Table of Contents

# Preface

Network administrators are facing an interesting challenge these days. On the one hand, computer networks are not something new anymore. They have been around for quite a while: their physical components and communication protocols are fairly well understood and don't represent a big mystery to an increasing number of professionals. Moreover, network appliances are getting cheaper and easier to set up, to the point that it doesn't take a certified specialist to install and configure a simple network or connect it to other networks. The very concept of networking is so widespread and ingrained in how users and developers think of a computer system that *being online* in some form is expected and taken for granted. In other words, a computer network is increasingly seen as a commodity.

On the other hand, the very same forces that are calling for *simpler, easier, accessible networks* are the ones that are actually pushing them to grow more and more complex every day. It's a matter of both quantity and quality. The number of connected devices on a given network is almost always constantly growing and so is the amount of data exchanged: media streams, application data, backups, database queries, and replication tend to saturate bandwidth just as much as they eat up storage space. As for quality, there are dozens of different requirements that factor in a given network setup: from having to manage different physical mediums (fiber, cable, radio, and so on), to the need to provide high performance and availability, both on the connection and on the application level; from the need to increase performance and reliability for geographical links, to providing confidentiality, security, and data integrity at all levels, and the list goes on.

These two contrasting, yet intertwined, tendencies are forcing network administrators to do more (more services, more availability, and more performance) with less (less budget, but also less attention from the management compared to newer, flashier technologies). Now, more than ever, as a network admin, you need to be able to keep an eye on your network in order to keep it in a healthy state, but also to quickly identify and resolve bottlenecks and outages of any kind—or better yet, find ways to anticipate and work around them before they happen. You'll also need to integrate your systems with different tools and environments (both legacy and strategic ones) that will be out of your direct control, such as asset databases, incident management systems, accounting and profiling systems, and so on. Even more importantly, you'll need to be able to show your work and explain your needs in clear, understandable terms to nontechnical people.

Now, if we were to say that Zabbix is the perfect, one-size-fits-all solution to all your network monitoring and management problems, we would clearly be lying. To this day, no such tool exists despite what many vendors want you to believe. Even if they have many features in common, when it comes to monitoring and capacity management, every network has its own quirks, special cases, and peculiar needs, to the point that any tool has to be carefully tuned to the environment or face the risk of becoming useless and neglected very quickly.

What is true is that Zabbix is a monitoring system powerful enough and flexible enough that, with the right amount of work, can be customized to meet your specific needs. And again, those needs are not limited to monitoring and alerting, but also to performance analysis and prediction, SLA reporting, and so on. When using Zabbix to monitor an environment, you can certainly create items that represent vital metrics for the network in order to have a real-time picture of what's happening. However, those same items can also prove very useful to analyze performance bottlenecks and to plan network expansion and evolution. Items, triggers, and actions can work together to let you take an active role in monitoring your network and easily identify and pre-empt critical outages.

In this book, we'll assume that you already know Zabbix as a general-purpose monitoring tool, and that you also used it to a certain extent. Specifically, we won't cover topics such as item, trigger, or action creation and configuration with a basic, step-by-step approach. Here, we want to focus on a few topics that could be of particular interest for network administrators, and we'll try to help them find their own answers to real-world questions such as the following:

- I have a large number of appliances to monitor and have to keep monitoring data available for a long time due to regulatory requirements. How do I install and configure Zabbix so that it is able to manage effectively this large amount of data?

- What are the best metrics to collect in order to both have an effective real-time monitoring solution and leverage historical data to make performance analysis and predictions?

- Many Zabbix guides and tutorials focus on using the Zabbix agent. The agent is certainly powerful and useful, but how do I leverage in an effective and secure way monitoring protocols that are already available on my network, such as SNMP and netflow?

- Load balancers, proxies, and web servers sometimes fall under a gray area between network and application administration. I have a bunch of web servers and proxies to monitor. What kind of metrics are most useful to check?

- I have a complex network with hosts that are deployed and decommissioned on a daily basis. How do I keep my monitoring solution up-to-date without resorting to long, error-prone manual interventions as much as possible?

- Now that I have collected a large amount of monitoring and performance data, how can I analyze it and show the results in a meaningful way? How do I put together the graphs I have available to show how they are related?

In the course of the next few chapters, we'll try to provide some pointers on how to answer those questions. We discuss as many practical examples and real-world applications as we can around the subject of network monitoring, but more than anything, we wanted to show you how it's relatively simple to leverage Zabbix's power and flexibility to your own needs.

The aim of this book is not to provide you with a set of prepackaged recipes and solutions that you can apply uncritically to your own environment. Even though we provided some scripts and code that are tested and working (and hopefully you'll find them useful), the real intention was always to give you a deeper understanding of the way Zabbix works so that you are able to create your own solutions to your own challenges.

We hope we have succeeded in our goal, and that by the end of the book, you'll find yourself a more confident network administrator and a more proficient Zabbix user. Even if this will not be the case, we hope you'll be able to find something useful in the following chapters: we touch upon different aspects of Zabbix and network monitoring and also discuss a couple of less known features that you might find very interesting nonetheless.

So, without further ado, let's get started with the actual content we want to show you.

# What this book covers

*Chapter 1, Installing a Distributed Zabbix Setup*, teaches you how to install Zabbix in a distributed setup, with a large use of proxies. The chapter will guide you through all the possible setup scenarios, showing you the main differences between the active and passive proxy setup. This chapter will explain how to prepare and set up a Zabbix installation, which is ready to be grown within your infrastructure, ready to support you, and monitor a large environment or even a very large one.

*Chapter 2, Active Monitoring of Your Devices*, offers you a few very useful examples of the different monitoring possibilities Zabbix can achieve by relying on different methods and protocols. You'll see how to query your network from the link level up to routing and network flow using ICMP, SNMP, and log-parsing facilities to collect your measurements. You will also learn how to extract meaningful information from the gathered data using aggregated and calculated items, and configuring complex triggers that will alert you about real network issues while minimizing signal noise and false positives.

*Chapter 3, Monitoring Your Network Services*, takes you through how to effectively monitor the most critical network services, such as DNS, DHCP, NTP, Apache proxy / reverse proxies, and proxy cache Squid. As it is easy to understand, all of them are critical services where a simple issue can affect your network setup and quickly propagate the issue to your entire network. You will understand how to extract meaningful metrics and useful data from all the listed services, being able then not only to monitor their own reliability, but also to acquire important metrics that can help you to predict failures or issues.

*Chapter 4, Discovering Your Network*, explains how to deeply automate the monitoring configuration of network objects. It will massively use the built-in discovery feature in order to keep the monitoring solution up-to-date within an evolving network environment. This chapter is divided into two core parts that cover the two main levels of Zabbix's discovery: host discovery and low-level discovery.

*Chapter 5, Visualizing Your Topology with Maps and Graphs*, shows you how to create complex graphs from your item's numerical values, automatically draw maps that reflect the current status of your network, and bring it all together using screens as a tool to customize monitoring data presentation. This chapter also presents a smart way to automate the initial startup of your Zabbix's setup, making you able to draw network diagrams using maps in a fully automated way. You will then learn a production-ready method to maintain maps while your network is growing or rapidly changing.

*Appendix A, Partitioning the Zabbix Database*, contains all the required software and stored procedures to efficiently partition your Zabbix database.

*Appendix B, Collecting Squid Metrics*, contains the software used to monitor Squid.

# What you need for this book

The software that has been used and is necessary for this book is:

- Linux Red Hat Enterprise Linux 6.5 or higher
- Zabbix 4.2
- Apache HTTPD 2.2
- MySQL Server-5.1
- Netflow 1.6.12
- Nmap

This book also requires an intermediate experience in shell scripting, a basic-to-intermediate knowledge of Python, and an intermediate knowledge of Zabbix.

Anyway, all the examples discussed and proposed in this book are explained well and commented upon. The same approach has been applied even to the software used on this book where it is explained, with a reasonable level of detail, how to set up and configure each software component.

# Who this book is for

This book is intended for experienced network administrators looking for a comprehensive monitoring solution for their networks. The reader must have a good knowledge of Unix/Linux, networking concepts, protocols, and appliances and a basic-to-intermediate knowledge of Zabbix. The reader will be guided step by step to manage and lead all the important points you will have to deal with. You will then be able to start up an effective and large-environment-ready Zabbix monitoring solution that will be a perfect fit within your network.

# Conventions

In this book, you will find a number of text styles that distinguish between different kinds of information. Here are some examples of these styles and an explanation of their meaning.

Code words in text, database table names, folder names, filenames, file extensions, pathnames, dummy URLs, user input, and Twitter handles are shown as follows: "On the Zabbix server-side, you need to carefully set the value of `StartTrappers=`."

A block of code is set as follows:

```
#First of all we need to import csv and Networkx
import csv
import networkx as nx
#Then we need to define who is our zabbix server and some other detail
to properly produce the DOT file
zabbix_service_ipaddr = "192.168.1.100"
main_loop_ipaddr = "10.12.20.1"
```

When we wish to draw your attention to a particular part of a code block, the relevant lines or items are set in bold:

```
# we can open our CSV file
csv_reader = csv.DictReader( open( 'my_export.csv' ), \
    delimiter=",", \
    fieldnames=( "ipaddress", "hostname", "oid", "dontcare",
"neighbors" ))
# Skip the header
csv_reader.next()
```

Any command-line input or output is written as follows:

```
# chkconfig --level 345 zabbix-server on
```

**New terms** and **important words** are shown in bold. Words that you see on the screen, for example, in menus or dialog boxes, appear in the text like this: "There is a clear warning on the website that warns us with this statement: **The Appliance is not intended for serious production use at this time**."

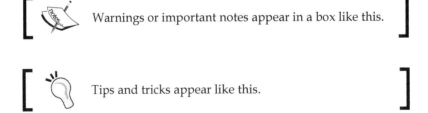

Warnings or important notes appear in a box like this.

Tips and tricks appear like this.

# Reader feedback

Feedback from our readers is always welcome. Let us know what you think about this book—what you liked or disliked. Reader feedback is important for us as it helps us develop titles that you will really get the most out of.

To send us general feedback, simply e-mail feedback@packtpub.com, and mention the book's title in the subject of your message.

If there is a topic that you have expertise in and you are interested in either writing or contributing to a book, see our author guide at www.packtpub.com/authors.

# Customer support

Now that you are the proud owner of a Packt book, we have a number of things to help you to get the most from your purchase.

# Downloading the example code

You can download the example code files from your account at http://www.packtpub.com for all the Packt Publishing books you have purchased. If you purchased this book elsewhere, you can visit http://www.packtpub.com/support and register to have the files e-mailed directly to you.

# Errata

Although we have taken every care to ensure the accuracy of our content, mistakes do happen. If you find a mistake in one of our books—maybe a mistake in the text or the code—we would be grateful if you could report this to us. By doing so, you can save other readers from frustration and help us improve subsequent versions of this book. If you find any errata, please report them by visiting http://www.packtpub.com/submit-errata, selecting your book, clicking on the **Errata Submission Form** link, and entering the details of your errata. Once your errata are verified, your submission will be accepted and the errata will be uploaded to our website or added to any list of existing errata under the Errata section of that title.

To view the previously submitted errata, go to https://www.packtpub.com/books/content/support and enter the name of the book in the search field. The required information will appear under the **Errata** section.

# Piracy

Piracy of copyrighted material on the Internet is an ongoing problem across all media. At Packt, we take the protection of our copyright and licenses very seriously. If you come across any illegal copies of our works in any form on the Internet, please provide us with the location address or website name immediately so that we can pursue a remedy.

Please contact us at `copyright@packtpub.com` with a link to the suspected pirated material.

We appreciate your help in protecting our authors and our ability to bring you valuable content.

# Questions

If you have a problem with any aspect of this book, you can contact us at `questions@packtpub.com`, and we will do our best to address the problem.

# 1
# Installing a Distributed Zabbix Setup

Most likely, if you are reading this book, you have already used and installed Zabbix as a network monitoring solution. Now, in this chapter, we will see how to install Zabbix in a distributed setup, eventually moving on to a large use of proxies. The chapter will take you through all the possible scenarios and explain the main differences between the active and passive proxy setup. Usually, the first Zabbix installation is done as a part of the concept to see whether the platform is good enough for you. Here, the common error is to start using this setup on a large production environment. After reading this chapter, you will be ready to install and set up a large environment ready infrastructure.

In this chapter, we will explain how to prepare and set up a Zabbix installation, which is ready to be grown within your infrastructure, and ready for a large to a very large environment. This book is mainly focused on Zabbix for network monitoring. This chapter will quickly take you through the installation process, emphasizing on all the most important points you need to consider. In the next chapter, we will spend more time describing a better approach to monitor your network devices and how to retrieve all the critical metrics from them. After reading this chapter, you will become aware of the communication between server and proxies being able to mix the active and passive setup in order to improve your infrastructure. You can extend the strong central Zabbix core setup with many lightweight and effective Zabbix proxies acting as a satellite inside your network to improve your monitoring system.

# Zabbix architectures

Zabbix was born as a distributed network monitoring tool with a central web interface where you can manage almost everything. Nowadays, with Zabbix 2.4, the number of possible architectures has been reduced to a single server setup and a Zabbix-proxies distributed setup.

 From Zabbix 2.4, the node-setup was discontinued. More information is available at https://www.zabbix.com/documentation/2.4/ manual/introduction/whatsnew240#node-based_ distributed_monitoring_removed.

Now, the simplest architecture (which is ready to handle large environments successfully) that you can implement composes of three servers:

- Web server
- RDBMS server
- Zabbix server

To prepare this simple setup for a large environment setting, it's better to use a dedicated server for each one of these components.

This is the simplest setup that can be easily extended and is ready to support a large environment.

The proposed architecture is shown in the following diagram:

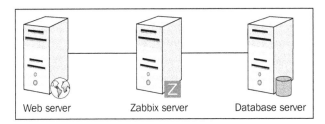

This kind of setup can be extended by adding many Zabbix proxies resulting in a proxy-based setup. The proxy-based setup is implemented with one Zabbix server and several proxies: one proxy per branch, data center or, in our case, for each remote network segment you need to monitor.

This configuration is easy to maintain and offers the advantage to have a centralized monitoring solution. This kind of configuration is the right balance between large environment monitoring and complexity.

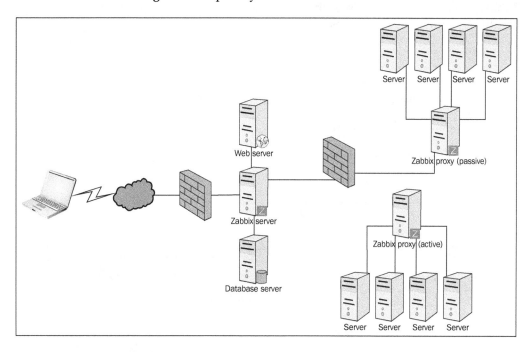

The Zabbix proxy, like a server, is used to collect data from any number of hosts or devices, acquiring all the metrics requested and acting as a proxy. This means that it can retain this data for an arbitrary period of time, relying on a dedicated database to do so. The proxy doesn't have a frontend and is managed directly from the central server.

> The proxy limits itself to data collection without trigger evaluations or actions; all the data is stored in its database. For this reason, it's better to use an efficient robust RDBMS that can prevent data loss in case of a crash.

All these characteristics make the Zabbix proxy a lightweight tool to deploy and offload some checks from the central server. Our objective is to control and streamline the flow of monitored data across networks, and the Zabbix proxy gives us the possibility to split and segregate items and data on the different networks. The most important feature is that the acquired metrics are stored in its database. Therefore, in case of a network loss, you will not lose them.

# Understanding Zabbix data flow

The standard Zabbix data flow is composed of several actors that send data to our Zabbix server. Of all the sources that can send data to our Zabbix server, we can identify three main data sources:

- Zabbix agent
- Zabbix sender
- Other agents (external scripts or components built in house)

The other agents represented in the next diagram can be of two main types:

- Custom and/or third-party agents
- Zabbix proxy

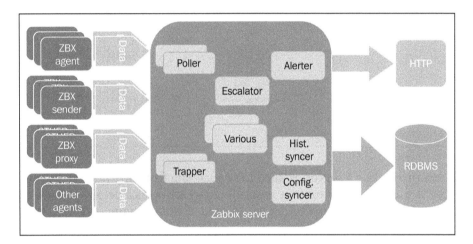

As the diagram displays the data that gets acquired from many different sources in the form of items. At the end of the diagram, you see the GUI, which practically represents the users connected and the database that is the place where all the values are stored.

In the next section, we will dive deep into the Zabbix proxies' data flow.

# Understanding the Zabbix proxies' data flow

Zabbix proxies can operate in two different modes, active and passive. The default setup is the active proxy. In this setup, the proxy initiates all connections to the Zabbix server, the one used to retrieve configuration information on monitored objects, and the connection to send measurements back to the server. Here, you can change and tweak the frequency of these two activities by setting the following variables in the proxy configuration file: /etc/zabbix/zabbix_proxy.conf:

```
ConfigFrequency=3600
DataSenderFrequency=1
```

Values are expressed in seconds. On the Zabbix server-side, you need to carefully set the value of StartTrappers=.

This value needs to be greater than the number of all active proxies and nodes you deployed. The trapper processes, indeed, manage all the incoming information from the proxies.

 Please note that the server will fork extra processes as required, if needed, but it is strongly advisable to prefork all the processes that are needed during the startup. This will reduce the overhead during the normal operation.

On the proxy side, another parameter to consider is:

```
HeartbeatFrequency
```

This parameter sets a sort of keep alive, which after the defined number of seconds, will contact the server although it doesn't have any data to send. The proxy availability can be easily checked with the following item:

```
zabbix[proxy, "proxy unique name", lastaccess]
```

Here the proxy unique name, of course, is the identifier you assigned to the proxy during deployment. The item will return the number of seconds as the last time that the proxy was contacted, a value you can then use with the appropriate triggering functions.

It's really important to have a trigger associated to this item, so you can be warned in case of connection loss. Looking at the trend of this trigger, you can learn about an eventual reaping time set on the firewall. Let's look at a practical example: if you notice that after 5 minutes your connections are dropped, set the heartbeat frequency to 120 seconds and check for the last access time above 300 seconds.

In the following diagram, you can see the communication flow between the Zabbix server and the proxy:

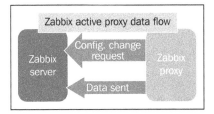

As you can see from the diagram, the server will wait to receive requests from the proxy and nothing more.

The active proxy is the most efficient way to offload duties from the server. Indeed, the server will just sit here waiting to be asked about changes in configuration, or to receive new monitoring data.

On the other side, proxies are usually deployed to monitor secure network segments with strict outgoing traffic policies, and are usually installed on DMZs. In these kind of scenarios, normally, it is very difficult to obtain permission for the proxy to initiate the communication with the server. Unfortunately, it's not just due to policies. DMZs are isolated as much as possible from internal networks, as they need to be as secure as they can. Generally, it's often easier and more accepted from a security point of view to initiate a connection from the internal network to a DMZ. In this kind of scenario, the passive proxy is very helpful. The passive proxy is almost a mirrored image of the active proxy setup, as you can see in the following diagram:

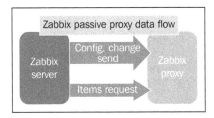

With this configuration, the Zabbix server will contact the proxy periodically to deliver the configuration changes and to request the item values the proxy is holding.

This is the proxy configuration to enable the proxy you need to set:

```
ProxyMode=1
```

This parameter specifies the passive proxy, you don't need to do anything else. Now, on the server side, you need to set the following parameters:

- `StartProxyPollers=`

  This will set the number of processes dedicated to the passive proxies

 The `StartProxyPollers` parameter should match the number of passive proxies you have deployed.

- `ProxyConfigFrequency=`

  This value expresses the frequency with which the server sends the configuration to its proxy

- `ProxyDataFrequency=`

  This is the interval parameter that expresses the number of seconds between two consecutive requests to get the acquired metrics from the proxy

The item used to check a passive proxy's availability is as follows:

```
zabbix[proxy, "proxy unique name", lastaccess]
```

This is exactly the same as the active one.

The passive proxy enables us to gather monitoring data from otherwise closed and locked down networks with a slightly increased overhead.

 You can mix as many active and passive proxies as you want in your environment. This enables you to expand your monitoring solution to reach each part of the network and to handle a large number of monitored objects. This approach keeps the architecture simple and easy to manage with a strong central core and many simple, lightweight satellites.

If you would like to keep track of all the remaining items that the proxy needs to send, you can set up the proxy to run this query against its database:

```
SELECT ((SELECT MAX(proxy_history.id) FROM proxy_history)-nextid)
  FROM ids WHERE field_name='history_lastid'
```

**Downloading the example code**

You can download the example code files from your account at
http://www.packtpub.com for all the Packt Publishing books
you have purchased. If you purchased this book elsewhere, you
can visit http://www.packtpub.com/support and register
to have the files e-mailed directly to you.

This query will return the number of items that the proxy still needs to send to the Zabbix server. Considering that you are using MySQL as a database, you need to add the following user parameter in the proxy agent configuration file:

```
UserParameter=zabbix.proxy.items.sync.remaining, mysql -u <your
  dbname here> -p '<your password here>' -e 'SELECT ((SELECT
  MAX(proxy_history.id) FROM proxy_history)-nextid) FROM ids WHERE
  field_name=history_lastid' 2>&1
```

Now, all you need to do is set an item on the Zabbix server side and you can see how your proxy is freeing its queue.

# Installing Zabbix

Zabbix, like all the other software, can be installed in two ways:

1. Download the latest source code and compile it.
2. Install it from packages.

Actually, there is another way to have a Zabbix server up and running: using the virtual appliance. The Zabbix server appliance will not be considered in this book as Zabbix itself defines this virtual appliance as *not ready* for productive environments. This virtual appliance is not a production ready setup for many reasons:

- It is a monolith where everything is installed on the same server.
- There is no separation from the database layer and the presentation layer. This means that each one of these components can affect the performance of the other.
- There is a clear warning on the website that warns us with this statement: **The Appliance is not intended for serious production use at this time**.

On the other hand, the installation from packages gives us some benefits:

- The packages make it easy to upgrade and update
- Dependencies are automatically sorted out

The source code compilation also gives us some benefits:

- We can compile only the needed features
- We can build the agent statically and deploy on different Linux *flavors*
- Complete control on update

It's quite usual to have different versions of Linux, Unix, and Microsoft Windows on a large environment. This kind of scenario is quite diffused on a heterogeneous infrastructure, and if we use the Zabbix's agent distribution package on each Linux server, we will have different versions of the agent for sure, and different locations for the configuration files.

The more the things are standardized across our server, the easier it will become to maintain and upgrade the infrastructure. The `--enable-static` option gives us a way to standardize the agent across different Linux versions and release, which is a strong benefit. The agent, statically compiled, can be easily deployed everywhere and, for sure, we will have the same location (and we can use the same configuration file apart from the node name) for the agent and his/her configuration file. The only thing that might vary is the start/stop script and how to register it on the right `init` runlevel, but at least the deployment will be standardized.

The same kind of concept can be applied to the commercial Unix, bearing in mind to compile it on the target environment so that the same agent can be deployed on different Unix releases of the same vendor.

# Installing from packages

The first thing to do to install Zabbix from repo is to add the yum repository to our list. This can be done with the following command:

```
$ rpm -Uvh http://repo.zabbix.com/zabbix/2.4/rhel/6/x86_64/zabbix-
release-2.4-1.el6.noarch.rpm
Retrieving http://repo.zabbix.com/zabbix/2.4/rhel/6/x86_64/zabbix-
release-2.4-1.el6.noarch.rpm
warning: /var/tmp/rpm-tmp.dsDB6k: Header V4 DSA/SHA1 Signature, key ID
79ea5ed4: NOKEY
Preparing...          ######################################### [100%]
1:zabbix-release      ######################################### [100%]
```

Once this is done, we can take advantage of all the benefits introduced by the package manager and have the dependencies automatically resolved by yum.

To install the Zabbix server, you simply need to run:

```
$ yum install zabbix-server-mysql zabbix-agent zabbix-javagateway
```

Now, you have your server ready to start. We can't start it now as we need to set up the database, which will be done in the next heading, anyway, what you can do is set up the start/stop runlevel for our `zabbix_server` and `zabbix_agent` daemons:

```
$ chkconfig --level 345 zabbix-server on
$ chkconfig --level 345 zabbix-agent on
```

Please double check if the previous command ran successfully with the following:

```
$ chkconfig --list | grep zabbix
zabbix-agent    0:off   1:off   2:off   3:on    4:on    5:on    6:off
zabbix-server   0:off   1:off   2:off   3:on    4:on    5:on    6:off
```

# Setting up a Zabbix agent

Now, as usually happens in a large server farm, it is possible that you have many different variants of Linux. Here, if you can't find the package for your distribution, you can even think to compile the agent from scratch. The following are the steps for the same:

1. Download the source code from the Zabbix website.
2. Unpack the software.
3. Satisfy all the software dependencies, installing all the related `-devel` packages.
4. Run the following command: `$ ./configure --enable-agent`.

> Here, you can statically link the produced binary with the `--enable-static` option. With this, the binary produced will not require any external library. This is really useful to distribute the agent across different versions of Linux.

Compile everything with `$ make`.

Now, before you run `$ make install`, you can decide to create your own package to distribute with CheckInstall.

# Creating a Zabbix agent package with CheckInstall

The advice is to not run `make install`, but use CheckInstall to produce the required package for your Linux OS from `http://asic-linux.com.mx/~izto/checkinstall/`.

 We can also use a prebuilt CheckInstall; the current release is `checkinstall-1.6.2-20.2.i686.rpm` on Red Hat / CentOS. The package will also need the rpm-build package:

**`rpm-build yum install`**

Also, we need to create the necessary directories:

`mkdir -p ~/rpmbuild/{BUILD,RPMS,SOURCES,SPECS,SRPMS}`

This software enables you to create a package for many different versions of the package manager, namely, RPM, deb, and `tgz`.

 CheckInstall will produce packages for Debian, Slackware, and Red Hat, helping us to prepare the Zabbix's agent package (statically linked) and distribute it around our server.

Now, we need to switch to the root account using `$ sudo su - `. Also, use the `checkinstall` followed by these options:

**`$ checkinstall --nodoc --install=yes -y`**

If you don't face any issue, you should get the following message:

```
*****************************************************************
Done. The new package has been saved to
/root/rpmbuild/RPMS/i386/zabbix-2.4.0-1.i386.rpm
You can install it in your system anytime using:
    rpm -i zabbix-2*.4.0-1.i386.rpm
*****************************************************************
```

Remember that the server binaries will be installed in `<prefix>/sbin`, utilities will be in `<prefix>/bin`, and the main pages under the `<prefix>/share` location.

 To specify a different location for Zabbix binaries, we need to use `--prefix` on the configure options (for example, `--prefix=/opt/zabbix`).

# Server configuration

For the server configuration, we only have one file to check and edit:

    /etc/zabbix/zabbix_server.conf

All the configuration files are contained in the following directory:

    /etc/zabbix/

All you need to change for the initial setup is the `/etc/zabbix/zabbix_server.conf` configuration file and write the username/password and database name here.

 Please take care to protect the access to the configuration file with `chmod 400 /etc/zabbix/zabbix_server.conf`.

The default external scripts location is:

    /usr/lib/zabbix/externalscripts

Also, the alert script directory is:

    /usr/lib/zabbix/alertscripts

This can be changed by editing the `zabbix_server.conf` file.

The configuration on the agent side is quite easy; basically, we need to write the IP address of our Zabbix server.

# Installing a database

The database we will use on this book, as already explained, is MySQL.

Now, considering that you have a Red Hat server, the procedure to install MySQL from the RPM repository is quite easy:

```
$ yum install mysql mysql-server
```

Now, you need to set up the MySQL service to start automatically when the system boots:

```
$ chkconfig --levels 235 mysqld on
$ /etc/init.d/mysqld start
```

Remember to set a password for the MySQL root user

To set a password for the root, you can run these two commands:

```
/usr/bin/mysqladmin -u root password 'new-password'
/usr/bin/mysqladmin -u root -h hostname-of-your.zabbix.db password 'new-password'
```

Alternatively, you can run:

```
/usr/bin/mysql_secure_installation
```

This will also help you to remove the test databases and anonymous user data that was created by default. This is strongly recommended for production servers.

Now, it's time to create the Zabbix database. For this, we can use the following commands:

```
$ mysql -u root -p
$ mysql> CREATE DATABASE zabbix CHARACTER SET UTF8;
Query OK, 1 row affected (0.00 sec)
$ mysql> GRANT ALL PRIVILEGES on zabbix.* to 'zabbixuser'@'localhost'
IDENTIFIED BY 'zabbixpassword';
Query OK, 0 rows affected (0.00 sec)
$ mysql> FLUSH PRIVILEGES;
$ mysql> quit
```

Next, we need to restore the default Zabbix MySQL database files:

```
$ mysql -u zabbixuser -pzabbixpassword zabbix< /usr/share/doc/zabbix-
server-mysql-2.4.0/create/schema.sql
$ mysql -u zabbixuser -pzabbixpassword zabbix < /usr/share/doc/zabbix-
server-mysql-2.4.0/create/images.sql
$ mysql -u zabbixuser -pzabbixpassword zabbix < /usr/share/doc/zabbix-
server-mysql-2.4.0/create/data.sql
```

Now, our database is ready. Before we begin to play with the database, it's important to do some consideration about database size and heavy tasks against it.

# Considering the database size

Zabbix uses two main groups of tables to store its data:

- History
- Trends

Now, the space consumed by these tables is influenced by:

- **Items**: This is the number of items you're going to acquire
- **Refresh rate**: This is the mean average refresh rate of our items
- **Space to store values**: This depends on RDBMS

The space used to store data can vary due to the database, but we can resume the space used by these tables in the following table:

| Type of measure | Retention in days | Space required |
|---|---|---|
| History | 30 | 10.8 G |
| Events | 1825 (5 years) | 15.7 GB |
| Trends | 1825 (5 years) | 26.7 GB |
| Total | NA | 53.2 GB |

This calculation is, of course, done considering the environment after 5 years of retention. Anyway, we need to have an environment ready to survive this period of time and retain the same shape that it had when it was installed. We can easily change the history and trends retention policy per item. This means that we can create a template with items that have a different history retention by default. Normally, the history is set to 30 days, but for some kind of measure (such as in web scenarios) or other particular measures, we need to keep all the values for more than a week. This permits us to change this value on each item.

# MySQL partitioning

Now that we are aware of how big our database will be, it's easy to imagine that housekeeping will be a heavy task and the time, CPU, and resource consumed by this one will grow together with the database size.

Housekeeping is in charge to remove the outdated metrics from the database and the information deleted by a user, and as we've seen the history, trends, and events tables are, after some time, huge tables. This explains why the process is so heavy to manage.

The only way we can improve performances once we have reached this volume of data is by using partitioning and disabling the housekeeper altogether.

Partitioning the history and trend tables will provide us with many major benefits:

- All history data in a table for a particular defined window time are self-contained in its own partition. This allows you to easily delete old data without impacting the database performance.

- When you use MySQL with InnoDB, and if you delete data contained in a table, the space is not released. The space freed is marked as free, but the disk space consumed will not change. When you use partition, and if you drop a partition, the space is immediately freed.

- Query performance can be improved dramatically in some situations, in particular, when there is heavy access to the table's rows in a single partition.

- When a query updates a huge amount of data or needs access to a large percentage of the partition, the sequential scan is often more efficient than the index usage with a random access or scattered reads against this index.

Unfortunately, Zabbix is not able to manage the partitions. So, we need to disable housekeeping, and use an external process to accomplish housekeeping.

What we need to have is a stored procedure that does all the work for us.

The following is the stored procedure:

```
DELIMITER $$
CREATE PROCEDURE `partition_maintenance`(SCHEMA_NAME VARCHAR(32),
    TABLE_NAME VARCHAR(32), KEEP_DATA_DAYS INT, HOURLY_INTERVAL INT,
    CREATE_NEXT_INTERVALS INT)
BEGIN
    DECLARE OLDER_THAN_PARTITION_DATE VARCHAR(16);
    DECLARE PARTITION_NAME VARCHAR(16);
    DECLARE LESS_THAN_TIMESTAMP INT;
    DECLARE CUR_TIME INT;
```

Until here, we have declared the variable we need after. Now, on the next line, we will call the stored procedure responsible to check whether a partition is already present and if not, we will create them:

```
CALL partition_verify(SCHEMA_NAME, TABLE_NAME,
    HOURLY_INTERVAL);
SET CUR_TIME = UNIX_TIMESTAMP(DATE_FORMAT(NOW(), '%Y-%m-%d
    00:00:00'));
IF DATE(NOW()) = '2014-04-01' THEN
```

```
        SET CUR_TIME = UNIX_TIMESTAMP(DATE_FORMAT(DATE_ADD
          (NOW(), INTERVAL 1 DAY), '%Y-%m-%d 00:00:00'));
    END IF;
    SET @__interval = 1;
    create_loop: LOOP
      IF @__interval > CREATE_NEXT_INTERVALS THEN
        LEAVE create_loop;
      END IF;
    SET LESS_THAN_TIMESTAMP = CUR_TIME + (HOURLY_INTERVAL *
      @__interval * 3600);
    SET PARTITION_NAME = FROM_UNIXTIME(CUR_TIME +
      HOURLY_INTERVAL * (@__interval - 1) * 3600,
      'p%Y%m%d%H00');
```

Now that we have calculated all the parameters needed by the `create_partition` procedure, we can run it. This stored procedure will create the new partition on the defined schema:

```
        CALL partition_create(SCHEMA_NAME, TABLE_NAME,
          PARTITION_NAME, LESS_THAN_TIMESTAMP);
        SET @__interval=@__interval+1;
    END LOOP;
    SET OLDER_THAN_PARTITION_DATE=DATE_FORMAT(DATE_SUB(NOW(),
      INTERVAL KEEP_DATA_DAYS DAY), '%Y%m%d0000');
```

The section that follows is responsible to remove the older partitions, using the `OLDER_TAN_PARTITION_DATE` procedure, which we have calculated on the lines before:

```
        CALL partition_drop(SCHEMA_NAME, TABLE_NAME,
          OLDER_THAN_PARTITION_DATE);
    END$$
    DELIMITER ;
```

This stored procedure will be the core of our housekeeping. It will be called with the following syntax:

```
CALL partition_maintenance('<zabbix_db_name>', '<table_name>',
  <days_to_keep_data>, <hourly_interval>,
  <num_future_intervals_to_create>)
```

The procedure works based on 1 hour intervals. Next, if you want to partition on a daily basis, the interval will be 24 hours. Instead, if you want 1 hour partitioning, the interval will be 1.

You need to specify the number of intervals that you want created in advance. For example, if you want 2 weeks interval of future partitions, use 14. If your interval is 1 (for hourly partitioning), then the number of intervals to create is 336 (24*14).

This stored procedure uses some other stores procedures:

- `partition_create`: This creates the partition for the specified table
- `partition_verify`: This checks whether the partition is enabled on a table, if not, then create a single partition
- `partition_drop`: This drops partitions older than a timestamp

For all the details about these stored procedures, see *Appendix A, Partitioning the Zabbix Database*.

Once you've created all the required stored procedures, you need to change two indexes to enable them in order to be ready for a partitioned table:

```
mysql> Alter table history_text drop primary key, add index (id), drop
index history_text_2, add index history_text_2 (itemid, id);
Query OK, 0 rows affected (0.49 sec)
Records: 0  Duplicates: 0  Warnings: 0


mysql> Alter table history_log drop primary key, add index (id), drop
index history_log_2, add index history_log_2 (itemid, id);
Query OK, 0 rows affected (2.71 sec)
Records: 0  Duplicates: 0  Warnings: 0
```

Once this is done, you need to schedule the `partition_maintenance_all` stored procedure with a cron job. For more details about the `partition_maintenance_all` procedure, please check the instructions contained in *Appendix A, Partitioning the Zabbix Database*. The cron job needs to execute the following command:

```
mysql -h <zabbix_db_host> -u<zabbixuser> -p<zabbixpassword>
zabbixdatabase -e "CALL partition_maintenance_all('zabbix');"
```

Once this has been set, you need to bear in mind to disable the housekeeping for history and trends. Verify that the **Override item <trend/history> period** Zabbix configuration is checked for both history and trends. Here, you need to set the **Data storage period (in days)** box for history and trends to the value you've defined in your procedure, our example in *Appendix A, Partitioning the Zabbix Database* is of 28 and 730.

# Installing a Zabbix proxy

Installation of the Zabbix proxy from packages is a quite simple task. Once you've added the Zabbix repository, you only need to run the following command:

```
$ yum install zabbix-proxy-mysql
```

This will install the required packages:

```
Installation:
 zabbix-proxy-mysql  x86_64  2.4.0-1.el6  zabbix  390 k
Installing for dependencies:
zabbix-proxy  x86_64  2.4.0-1.el6  zabbix  21 k
```

The Zabbix proxy installation is quite similar to the server one. Once you've installed the server, you need to install MySQL, create the database, and import the DB schema:

```
$ mysql -u root -p
$ mysql> CREATE DATABASE zabbix CHARACTER SET UTF8;
Query OK, 1 row affected (0.00 sec)
$ mysql> GRANT ALL PRIVILEGES on zabbix.* to 'zabbixuser'@'localhost'
IDENTIFIED BY 'zabbixpassword';
Query OK, 0 rows affected (0.00 sec)
$ mysql> FLUSH PRIVILEGES;
$ mysql> quit
```

Next, we need to restore the default Zabbix MySQL database files:

```
$ mysql -u zabbixuser -pzabbixpassword zabbix < /usr/share/doc/zabbix-
proxy-mysql-2.4.0/create/schema.sql
```

Now, we need to start the database, configure the proxy, and start the service. In this example, we have considered to use a Zabbix proxy that relies on a MySQL with InnoDB database. This proxy can be performed in two different ways:

- Lightweight (and then use SQLite3)
- Robust and solid (and then use MySQL)

Here, we have chosen the second option. In a large network environment where the proxy, in case of issue, needs to preserve all the metrics acquired until the server acquires the metrics, it's better to reduce, at the minimum, the risk of data loss. Also, if you consider this scenario in a large network environment, you most likely will have thousands of subnetworks connected to the Zabbix server with all the possible network devices in-between. Well, exactly, this is necessary to use a database that can prevent any data corruptions.

# Installing the WebGUI interface

The WebGUI interface will be done once more using the RPMs.

To install the web interface, you need to run the following command:

```
$ yum install zabbix-web-mysql
```

Yum will take care to resolve all the dependencies. Once you're done, the process of this component is quite easy: we need to open a web browser, point at the following URL: `http://your-web-server/zabbix`, and follow the instructions.

On the standard Red Hat system, you simply need to change these parameters on your `/etc/php.ini` file:

```
php_value max_execution_time 300
php_value memory_limit 128M
php_value post_max_size 16M
php_value upload_max_filesize 2M
php_value max_input_time 300
```

Also, set your time zone on the same file (for example, `php_value date.timezone Europe/Rome`).

Now, it's time to start up Apache, but before this, we need to check whether we have SELinux enabled and on which mode? To check your SELinux status, you can run:

```
# sestatus
SELinux status:              enabled
SELinuxfs mount:             /selinux
Current mode:                permissive
Mode from config file:       permissive
Policy version:              24
Policy from config file:     targeted
```

Now, you need to check whether you have the httpd daemon enabled to use the network with the following command:

```
# getsebool httpd_can_network_connect
httpd_can_network_connect --> off
```

Most likely, you will have the same kind of result, then all we need to do is enable the httpd_can_network_connect option using the next command with -P to preserve the value after a reboot:

```
# setsebool -P httpd_can_network_connect on
# getsebool httpd_can_network_connect
httpd_can_network_connect --> on
```

Now, all that we still have to do is enable the httpd daemon and start our httpd server:

```
# service httpd start
Starting httpd:                                    [  OK  ]
```

Next, enable the httpd server as a service:

```
    # chkconfig httpd on
```

We can check the change done with the next command:

```
# chkconfig --list httpd
httpd           0:off   1:off   2:on    3:on    4:on    5:on    6:off
```

Once you've done this, you only need to follow the wizard, and in a few clicks, you will have your web interface ready to start up.

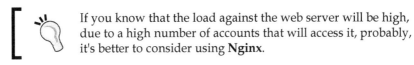

> If you know that the load against the web server will be high, due to a high number of accounts that will access it, probably, it's better to consider using **Nginx**.

Now, you can finally start your Zabbix server and the first entry in the /var/log/zabbix/zabbix_server.log file will look something like the following code:

```
37909:20140925:091128.868 Starting Zabbix Server. Zabbix 2.4.0 (revision 48953).
37909:20140925:091128.868 ****** Enabled features ******
 37909:20140925:091128.868 SNMP monitoring:           YES
 37909:20140925:091128.868 IPMI monitoring:           YES
 37909:20140925:091128.868 WEB monitoring:            YES
```

```
37909:20140925:091128.868 VMware monitoring:          YES
37909:20140925:091128.868 Jabber notifications:       YES
37909:20140925:091128.868 Ez Texting notifications:   YES
37909:20140925:091128.868 ODBC:                       YES
37909:20140925:091128.868 SSH2 support:               YES
37909:20140925:091128.868 IPv6 support:               YES
37909:20140925:091128.868 ******************************
37909:20140925:091128.868 using configuration file: /etc/zabbix/zabbix_
server.conf******************************
```

Next, you can start to implement and acquire all the items critical for your network.

# Summary

In this chapter, we covered a large number of components. We started with defining what a large environment is. We also saw how the network setup can be designed and how it can evolve within your infrastructure. We saw the heaviest task on the server side (housekeeping) and how to avoid performance degradation due to this. We discussed MySQL partitioning in-depth. We also briefly discussed the differences between active and passive proxies; you will now be able to decide how to set them up and which one to choose once you know your network topology. Also, we saw how to acquire some critical metrics to monitor the Zabbix proxy connection and the amount of items that it still needs to send us.

As you can see, we covered a lot of arguments in just one chapter; we did this because we would like to use more space in the upcoming chapters. In the next chapter, we will explore the different appliances and protocols at layer 2 and layer 3 of the ISO/OSI stack. Also, you will see how to best extrapolate meaningful monitoring data from the collected measure for the protocol layers 2 and 3.

# 2
# Active Monitoring of Your Devices

Now that you have a working Zabbix setup, it's time to take a look at your network and figure out the components that you want to monitor, the kind of data you want to collect, and the conditions under which you want to be notified about problems and state changes.

It would be impossible for any book on this topic to fully cover all the different kinds of network appliances and topologies and all the different monitoring scenarios that a network administrator might need as every environment has its own specific quirks that a good monitoring solution has to account for. This chapter will offer you a few examples of the different monitoring possibilities Zabbix can achieve by relying on different methods and protocols. You'll see how to query your network from the data link layer up to routing and network flow using ICMP, SNMP, and log parsing facilities to collect your measurements.

You'll learn how to extract meaningful information from the data you gathered using aggregated and calculated items and how to configure complex triggers that will alert you about real network issues while minimizing uninteresting or nonrelevant data.

By the end of the chapter, you'll have a good overview of Zabbix's network monitoring possibilities, and you'll be ready to adapt what you learned for your specific requirements. But let's first have a quick overview of how Zabbix organizes monitoring data with hosts, templates, items, and triggers.

# Understanding Zabbix hosts

One of Zabbix's great strengths is its flexibility when it comes to organizing monitoring data. Even without considering its powerful templating and discovery features, which will be covered in *Chapter 4, Discovering Your Network*, there is a lot that you can do with standard hosts, items, and triggers. Here are a few tips on how you can use them effectively.

## Hosts and host groups

Zabbix hosts usually represent a single, specific box or appliance in your network. They can also be a part of one or more host groups.

Host groups are very useful as they make it easy to navigate Zabbix's interface, separating hosts into categories and allowing you to organize and manage a huge amount of appliances without having to deal with impossibly long lists of hostnames. The same host can be part of different host groups, and this can be very useful as you might want, for example, to have a group for all your routers, a group for all your switches, and a group for every subnet you manage. So, a single router will be part of the *routers* group and all the *subnet* groups it has an interface on, while a switch will be part of the *switches* group and of the *subnet* it's part of, and so on.

While this is certainly a good way to organize your hosts, both to visualize and to manage your monitoring data, there are a couple of not-too-obvious pitfalls you should be aware of if you decide to put the same host in multiple groups:

- Calculated items show aggregate monitoring data based on host group membership. If you configure an aggregated item that uses more than one calculated item from different host groups, you can end up using the same host's data more than once, introducing a significant error in your calculations.

- Actions are usually filtered based on host groups. This means that the same trigger event could fire up more than one action if the host is part of more than one host group, leading to potentially duplicate messages and alerts.

- User access permissions are host-group-based. This means that some users could be able to see more hosts and monitoring data than they actually need to if a host ends up in a host group they have access to.

This is by no means an attempt to discourage the practice of assigning multiple host groups to the same host. Just be aware of the ramifications of such a practice and don't forget to take into consideration the added complexity when you configure your items, actions, and access permissions.

# Host interfaces

Each host is composed of a collection of items that represent the raw monitoring data, and triggers, which represent Zabbix's monitoring intelligence based on the data gathered. It's also composed of a series of **interfaces** that tell the Zabbix server or proxy how to contact the host to collect the aforesaid monitoring data. Most network appliances have more than one interface, so you would want to make sure that all hosts that represent routers, firewalls, proxies, gateways, and whatnot, are listing all those appliances' interfaces and their addresses. The advantages are obvious:

- You'll be able to quickly review what addresses are configured on a specific host while looking at monitoring data

- You'll be able to differentiate your checks by querying different addresses or ports of the same host based on your needs

- Your maps and topologies will be more consistent with what's actually deployed

Adding interfaces to a host is fairly straightforward. All you need to do is navigate to **Configuration** | **Hosts** and then select the host you want to edit. The interfaces section is in the main configuration tab, as shown in the following screenshot:

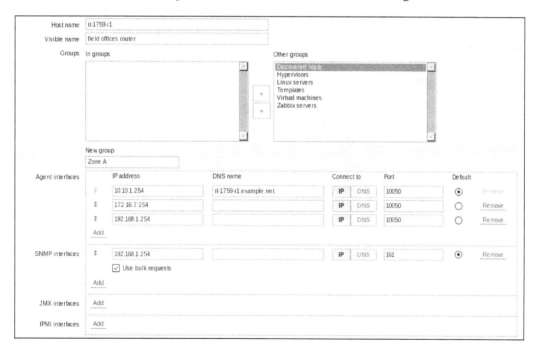

As you can see in the above example, there are three agent interfaces that show all the networks the router is connected to and just one SNMP interface. Agent interfaces are used not only for Zabbix agent items, but also for simple and external checks. On the other hand, you'll use SNMP interfaces to send SNMP queries to your host. The preceding example assumes that you'll only use SNMP on the router's interface that is connected to a management network (192.168.1.0 in this example), while you'll also use ICMP, TCP, and external checks on its two production interfaces. Of course, you are free to configure different IP addresses for Agent and SNMP interfaces depending on what protocols and checks you plan to activate on which interfaces.

# Host inventory

Having inventory data directly available in your monitoring solution has a lot of obvious advantages when it comes to attaching useful information to your alerts and alarms. Unfortunately, the more hosts you have to manage, the more essential it is to have up-to-date inventory information, and the harder it is to maintain the aforesaid information in a reliable and timely manner. Manually updating a host's inventory data can quickly become an impossible task when you have tens or hundreds of hosts to manage, and it's not always possible to write automated scripts that will do the job for you. Fortunately, Zabbix offers an automatic inventory feature that can at least partially fill in inventory data based on actual monitoring data. To activate this feature, first you'll need to select **Automatic** in the **Host inventory** tab of a host configuration page and then move to the items that you'll use to populate the inventory data.

When configuring an item, you should assign its data to a specific inventory field so that the aforesaid field's value will be set and automatically updated based on the item's measurements, as shown in the following screenshot:

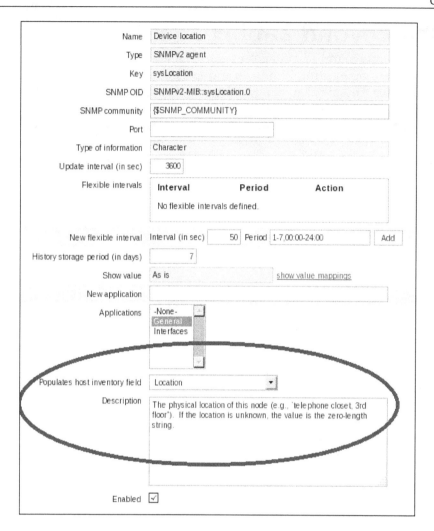

As you can see in the preceding example, a host's location inventory value will be populated based on the corresponding SNMP query. This means that if you change a device's location information, that change will be reflected in Zabbix as soon as the item's value is polled on the device. Depending on the data available on the device, you'll be able to populate only a few inventory fields or most of them, while falling back on manual updates of the fields that fall outside of your device's reporting possibilities.

Speaking of items, let's now focus on the different monitoring possibilities that Zabbix items offer and how to apply them to your environment.

# Going beyond Zabbix agents

There are certainly many advantages in using Zabbix's own agents and protocol when it comes to monitoring Windows and Unix operating systems or the applications that run on them. However, when it comes to network monitoring, the vast majority of monitored objects are network appliances of various kinds, where it's often impossible to install and run a dedicated agent of any type. This by no means implies that you'll be unable to fully leverage Zabbix's power to monitor your network. Whether it's a simple ICMP echo request, an SNMP query, an SNMP trap, netflow logging, or a custom script, there are many possibilities to extract meaningful data from your network. This section will show you how to set up these different methods of gathering data, and give you a few examples on how to use them.

## Simple checks

Let's start with the simplest case. At first glance, simple checks don't look that interesting: excluding all the VMware Hypervisor checks that are included in this category, simple checks are reduced to a couple of generic TCP/IP connection checks and three ICMP echo checks, as follows:

| Check name | Description |
| --- | --- |
| Icmpping | This returns 1 if the host responds to an ICMP ping; 0 otherwise |
| Icmppingloss | This returns the percentage of lost ICMP ping packets |
| Icmppingsec | This returns the ICMP response time in seconds |
| Net.tcp.service | This returns 1 if the host accepts connections on a specified TCP port; 0 otherwise |
| Net.tcp.service.perf | This returns the number of seconds spent to obtain a connection on a specified TCP port |

Generally speaking, these checks prove more useful as the distance between the monitoring probe and the monitored host increases, both in terms of physical distance (a geographical link to another city for example) and in terms of hops a packet has to go through. This means that if you are interested in your network's performance, it would make sense to assign hosts with simple checks to Zabbix proxies that are *not* in the same subnet, but are situated where they will mimic as closely as possible your actual network traffic. Net.tcp.service is particularly useful from this point of view, not just to check the status of the availability of specific services when you cannot use Zabbix agents, but also to check general host availability across restrictive firewalls that block ICMP traffic.

In order to reduce network traffic and to make more efficient ICMP checks, Zabbix uses `fping` instead of the regular ping when executing `icmpping`, `icmppingloss`, and `icmppingsec` item checks.

Make sure you have `fping` installed on your Zabbix server and also on all the Zabbix proxies that might need it. If you don't have it, a simple `yum install fping` will usually be enough for the Zabbix daemons to find it and use it.

While both `net.tcp.service` and `net.tcp.service.perf` do support some well-known protocols, such as SSH, FTP, HTTP, and so on, these two items' most useful option is probably the one that allows you to perform a simple TCP handshake connection and check whether a specific IP is reachable on a specific port. These kind of checks are useful because, just like ICMP pings, they will mostly involve the network stack, reducing application overhead to a minimum, thus giving you data that more closely matches your actual network performance. On the other hand, unlike ICMP pings, they will allow you to check for TCP port availability for a given host. Obvious use cases include making lightweight service checks that will not impact very busy hosts or appliances too much, and making sure that a given firewall is allowing traffic through.

A slightly less obvious use case is using one or more `net.tcp.service` items to make sure that some services are *not* running on a given interface. Take for example, the case of a border router or firewall. Unless you have some very special and specific needs, you'll typically want to make sure that no admin consoles are available on the external interfaces. You might have double-checked the appliance's initial configuration, but a system update, a careless admin, or a security bug might change the aforesaid configuration and open your appliance's admin interfaces to a far wider audience than intended. A security breach like this one could pass unobserved for a long time unless you configure a few simple TCP/IP checks on your appliance's external interfaces and then set up some triggers that will report a problem if those checks report an open and responsive port.

Let's take the example of the router with two production interfaces and a management interface shown in the section about host interfaces. If the router's HTTPS admin console is available on TCP port 8000, you'll want to configure a simple check item for every interface:

| Item name | Item key |
| --- | --- |
| management_https_console | net.tcp.service[https,192.168.1.254,8000] |
| zoneA_https_console | net.tcp.service[https,10.10.1.254,8000] |
| zoneB_https_console | net.tcp.service[https,172.16.7.254,8000] |

All these checks will return 1 if the service is available, and 0 if the service is not available. What changes is how you implement the triggers on these items. For the management item, you'll have a problem if the service is not available, while for the other two, you'll have a problem if the service is indeed available, as shown in the following table:

| Trigger name | Trigger expression |
| --- | --- |
| Management console down | {it-1759-r1:net.tcp.service[http,192.168.1.254,8000].last()}=0 |
| Console available from zone A | {it-1759-r1:net.tcp.service[http,10.10.1.254,8000].last()}=1 |
| Console available from zone B | {it-1759-r1:net.tcp.service[http,172.16.7.254,8000].last()}=1 |

This way, you'll always be able to make sure that your device's configuration when it comes to open or closed ports will always match your expected setup and be notified when it diverges from the standard you set.

To summarize, simple checks are great for all cases where you don't need complex monitoring data from your network as they are quite fast and lightweight. For the same reason, they could be the preferred solution if you have to monitor availability for hundreds to thousands of hosts as they will impart a relatively low overhead on your overall network traffic.

When you do need more structure and more detail in your monitoring data, it's time to move to the bread and butter of all network monitoring solutions: SNMP.

# Keeping SNMP simple

The **Simple Network Monitoring Protocol (SNMP)** is an excellent, general purpose protocol that has become widely used beyond its original purpose. When it comes to network monitoring though, it's also often the only protocol supported by many appliances, so it's often a forced, albeit natural and sensible, choice to integrate it into your monitoring scenarios. As a network administrator, you probably already know all there is to know about SNMP and how it works, so let's focus on how it's integrated into Zabbix and what you can do with it.

First of all, we'll need to talk about SNMP gets and SNMP traps in two different discussions as they are implemented and used in different ways by Zabbix. The reason for this separation is in the very nature of **SNMP gets** as opposed to **SNMP traps**. An **SNMP get** represents a single, discrete piece of information that represents the current status of a metric, and it's not tied to any specific event. Whether it's a counter with the total number of bytes that passed through an interface, a Boolean value that will tell if a link is up or down, or a string with an appliance's location or contact information, an SNMP value will be available at any moment, and it will be possible to poll it with an arbitrary frequency.

This maps nicely to Zabbix items. Just like SNMP get values, they also represent single, discrete values that can be polled with arbitrary frequency. This makes it really straightforward to use regular SNMP queries to populate Zabbix items since the only things you have to worry about are the SNMP OID, the data type, and the community string or authentication information. We'll see a few examples in the next paragraph.

An SNMP trap represents a specific event that happens at a specific point in time. It might represent a link state change, a reboot event, or a user login. In any case, you cannot query the state of an SNMP trap; you just have to wait to receive one, and it will not represent a single, discrete value but a change from one value to another. They resemble, in many ways, Zabbix events instead of raw data. This complicates things a little since Zabbix events are the result of evaluating triggers against collected data, while SNMP traps can only enter Zabbix as item values, that is, as collected data. So we'll need to resolve this apparent mismatch in order to fully leverage the information contained in SNMP traps. We'll see how in a short while, but first let's look at a few details concerning regular SNMP queries executed from Zabbix.

# Getting SNMP data into Zabbix

A Zabbix server usually comes with good SNMP support out of the box. Not only does it support the querying protocol natively, but it also comes equipped with a number of SNMP templates that can get you started in the right direction. This means that for most devices you only have to link the **Template SNMP Device** template, and you'll immediately be able to get some basic information about it, as shown in the following screenshot:

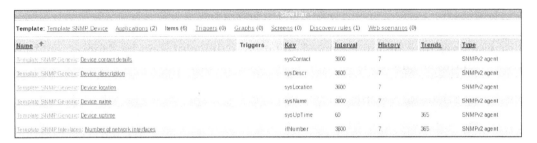

We've already seen how the **Device location** item can be used to populate a host's inventory location record, but there are a couple of other useful bits of information in the above picture.

First of all, there's a low-level discovery rule to explore. We'll delve more deeply into discovery rules in *Chapter 4, Discovering Your Network*, but for now, we'll just see that it's about dynamically creating network interface items:

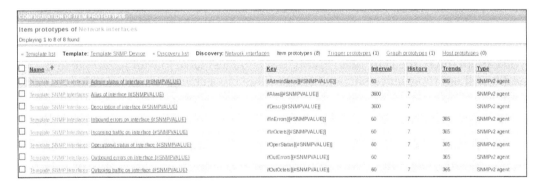

For every interface, eight items will be created, including the interface name, operational status, incoming and outgoing traffic, and so on. This means that the same template will be useful for the basic monitoring of network appliances with any number of network interfaces.

The second thing to notice, looking at both images, is the update interval, and history and trend retention periods for the items. Zabbix tries to set some sensible defaults, but you'll probably need to update some of those values based on the number of monitored hosts you have in your environment, your storage space availability, and the network load of your monitoring traffic.

> Another parameter that is related to Zabbix's performance is the initial (and minimum) number of pollers that the server keeps active at any given time. If you find that your polling queue is getting longer, you might want to increase the number of pollers in `zabbix_server.conf`. The available default options are:
>
> * `# StartPollers=5`
> * `# StartIPMIPollers=0`
> * `# StartPollersUnreachable=1`
> * `# StartTrappers=5`
> * `# StartPingers=1`
> * `# StartDiscoverers=1`
> * `# StartHTTPPollers=1`
>
> Work your way up slowly, or you'll just end up with unnecessary processes being created when Zabbix is started.

If you have hundreds of hosts to monitor, and for every host, you collect tens of single measurements every minute, you would reach a point where your Zabbix server's network load or CPU load will start to impact on the server's performance, leading to delays in item polling or dropped connections. If you cannot just upgrade to more powerful hardware, you might have to tweak the polling interval of your templates so that they strike a good balance between granularity of detail and performance.

A device's name, contact details, description, location, and such like, will rarely change once the device has been deployed, so it would be a waste to poll for those values every hour (3,600 seconds). By changing the interval to 6 hours or even a day, you'll automatically reduce your network traffic related to essentially fixed information by a factor of 6, up to 24.

Raising the polling interval for some of the interface counters can have an even more dramatic impact on your system and network load. While you'll probably want to check the admin and operational status of an interface as often as possible—otherwise you run the risk of not getting notified about possible problems in a timely manner—on the other hand, you'll probably be able to live with polling incoming and outgoing traffic and errors every five minutes (300 seconds) instead of every minute. Your graphs will still be very detailed, but your network will be much less flooded with SNMP requests. Keep in mind that changes like these might not seem much when referred to a single host, but as the number of your monitored objects grow, you can very quickly run up to hundreds or even thousands of new monitoring values per second coming into your Zabbix server.

The same can be said when it comes to retention periods and storage space. In this case, keep in mind that trends store about three values per hour (min, max and average) over the time range specified, while history stores all values collected in the specified time range. This means that based on your polling interval, it's usually cheaper to extend a trend retention value than a history one. This is, of course, valid only for numerical values as string ones can't really have trends, just history.

One last thing to notice in the above images is that the monitoring protocol for all items is set to SNMPv2. Just like SNMPv1, SNMPv2 doesn't offer real security for the monitoring data that crosses the network between an appliance and the monitoring server: all traffic is sent and received in the clear, and the SNMP community is just a string, easily parsable from intercepted traffic. While it's certainly true that a few network appliances don't support SNMPv3 because either they are too old or they are too simple, It's also true that the new version of the protocol has been around for quite a while now and a number of appliances do support it. The main advantages of SNMPv3 are its authentication and encryption capabilities. These can help make sure that all monitoring traffic is not bogus or corrupted, and that it's kept confidential from prying eyes. This is particularly important if you need to monitor some hosts over a network link you have no real control over, such as a WAN connection through a third-party provider. It would always be nice to use SNMPv3 across your network, but in cases like these, you are strongly encouraged to do so as there's a real possibility that your traffic can be indeed intercepted and tapped into.

Let's take the example of a Cisco router, and let's see how to configure SNMPv3 on it before moving on to the Zabbix side.

First of all, let's create a monitoring group. This is used to define access to the device's MIBs. On the Cisco router, open a console session and go into configuration mode. Then issue the following command:

```
R1(config)#snmp-server group MonitoringGroup v3 priv
```

The `v3` keyword specifies that we want to use SNMPv3, while the `priv` keyword specifies that we want to use both authentication and encryption. It's possible to pass more options to the preceding command in order to define an access list if you want to limit access to specific MiBs, but we'll keep things simple here and let our Zabbix probe access all MIBs.

Now that we have a group, we can create a user, as follows:

```
R1(config)#snmp-server user zabbix MonitoringGroup v3 auth sha zbxpass
priv aes 128 zbxpriv
```

As you can see, we assigned the Zabbix user to the previously created group and defined the authentication and encryption passphrases. Take note of all these elements as you'll need to specify all of them on Zabbix's side and they will need to match what you used here. To summarize, here is what you'll input later when configuring an SNMPv3 Zabbix item:

| Field | Value |
| --- | --- |
| User | `zabbix` |
| Authentication protocol | `sha` |
| Authentication passphrase | `zbxpass` |
| Privacy protocol | `aes` |
| Privacy passphrase | `zbxpriv` |

 Please don't use the passphrases shown here. These are intentionally weak, and we used them for illustration purposes only.

This is all there is to it. Later, we'll add some information about telling the appliance where to send SNMP traps, but for now you're ready to get SNMP values from your appliance, so let's focus on that for a while.

# Finding the right OIDs to monitor

While Zabbix's default SNMP templates will help you get started with basic monitoring, you'll soon find the need to poll your devices for more information. To do that, you'll need to know the OID of the metric you want to monitor as well as the data type it will yield. A first option is to consult your vendor's documentation on the device and find out which MIBs and OIDs are exposed by the SNMP agent. Another, more interactive, option is to find them using the `snmpwalk` utility and directly asking your device for them.

If you don't already have snmpwalk (and the other SNMP utilities for Linux) installed, you can quickly do so with a simple command:

`#yum install net-snmp-utils`

OIDs are sent and received by SNMP agents and servers as dotted sequences of numbers. Just like IP addresses, this is convenient for machine-to-machine communication, but hard to read for humans. In order to make the most from the exploration of your device using snmpwalk, make sure you have all the MIBs you need installed. MIBs essentially map OIDs to readable and understandable descriptions of themselves. In other words, they take output like this one:

```
.1.3.6.1.2.1.2.2.1.1.1 = INTEGER: 1
.1.3.6.1.2.1.2.2.1.1.2 = INTEGER: 2
.1.3.6.1.2.1.2.2.1.1.3 = INTEGER: 3
.1.3.6.1.2.1.2.2.1.1.5 = INTEGER: 5
.1.3.6.1.2.1.2.2.1.2.1 = STRING: lo
.1.3.6.1.2.1.2.2.1.2.2 = STRING: eth1
.1.3.6.1.2.1.2.2.1.2.3 = STRING: tap0
.1.3.6.1.2.1.2.2.1.2.5 = STRING: br0
.1.3.6.1.2.1.2.2.1.3.1 = INTEGER: softwareLoopback(24)
.1.3.6.1.2.1.2.2.1.3.2 = INTEGER: ethernetCsmacd(6)
.1.3.6.1.2.1.2.2.1.3.3 = INTEGER: ethernetCsmacd(6)
.1.3.6.1.2.1.2.2.1.3.5 = INTEGER: ethernetCsmacd(6)
.1.3.6.1.2.1.2.2.1.4.1 = INTEGER: 16436
.1.3.6.1.2.1.2.2.1.4.2 = INTEGER: 1500
.1.3.6.1.2.1.2.2.1.4.3 = INTEGER: 1500
.1.3.6.1.2.1.2.2.1.4.5 = INTEGER: 1500
.1.3.6.1.2.1.2.2.1.5.1 = Gauge32: 10000000
.1.3.6.1.2.1.2.2.1.5.2 = Gauge32: 1000000000
.1.3.6.1.2.1.2.2.1.5.3 = Gauge32: 10000000
.1.3.6.1.2.1.2.2.1.5.5 = Gauge32: 0
.1.3.6.1.2.1.2.2.1.6.1 = STRING:
.1.3.6.1.2.1.2.2.1.6.2 = STRING: 0:c:29:24:15:50
.1.3.6.1.2.1.2.2.1.6.3 = STRING: 2:10:f7:72:77:50
.1.3.6.1.2.1.2.2.1.6.5 = STRING: 0:c:29:24:15:50
.1.3.6.1.2.1.2.2.1.7.1 = INTEGER: up(1)
```

```
.1.3.6.1.2.1.2.2.1.7.2 = INTEGER: up(1)
.1.3.6.1.2.1.2.2.1.7.3 = INTEGER: up(1)
.1.3.6.1.2.1.2.2.1.7.5 = INTEGER: up(1)
.1.3.6.1.2.1.2.2.1.8.1 = INTEGER: up(1)
.1.3.6.1.2.1.2.2.1.8.2 = INTEGER: up(1)
.1.3.6.1.2.1.2.2.1.8.3 = INTEGER: up(1)
.1.3.6.1.2.1.2.2.1.8.5 = INTEGER: up(1)
```

Then, they turn it into a much more readable form:

```
IF-MIB::ifIndex.1 = INTEGER: 1
IF-MIB::ifIndex.2 = INTEGER: 2
IF-MIB::ifIndex.3 = INTEGER: 3
IF-MIB::ifIndex.5 = INTEGER: 5
IF-MIB::ifDescr.1 = STRING: lo
IF-MIB::ifDescr.2 = STRING: eth1
IF-MIB::ifDescr.3 = STRING: tap0
IF-MIB::ifDescr.5 = STRING: br0
IF-MIB::ifType.1 = INTEGER: softwareLoopback(24)
IF-MIB::ifType.2 = INTEGER: ethernetCsmacd(6)
IF-MIB::ifType.3 = INTEGER: ethernetCsmacd(6)
IF-MIB::ifType.5 = INTEGER: ethernetCsmacd(6)
IF-MIB::ifMtu.1 = INTEGER: 16436
IF-MIB::ifMtu.2 = INTEGER: 1500
IF-MIB::ifMtu.3 = INTEGER: 1500
IF-MIB::ifMtu.5 = INTEGER: 1500
IF-MIB::ifSpeed.1 = Gauge32: 10000000
IF-MIB::ifSpeed.2 = Gauge32: 1000000000
IF-MIB::ifSpeed.3 = Gauge32: 10000000
IF-MIB::ifSpeed.5 = Gauge32: 0
IF-MIB::ifPhysAddress.1 = STRING:
IF-MIB::ifPhysAddress.2 = STRING: 0:c:29:24:15:50
IF-MIB::ifPhysAddress.3 = STRING: 2:10:f7:72:77:50
IF-MIB::ifPhysAddress.5 = STRING: 0:c:29:24:15:50
IF-MIB::ifAdminStatus.1 = INTEGER: up(1)
IF-MIB::ifAdminStatus.2 = INTEGER: up(1)
IF-MIB::ifAdminStatus.3 = INTEGER: up(1)
```

```
IF-MIB::ifAdminStatus.5 = INTEGER: up(1)
IF-MIB::ifOperStatus.1 = INTEGER: up(1)
IF-MIB::ifOperStatus.2 = INTEGER: up(1)
IF-MIB::ifOperStatus.3 = INTEGER: up(1)
IF-MIB::ifOperStatus.5 = INTEGER: up(1)
```

If you have the right MIBs, you won't have to guess the meaning of each OID from its value as most of the time, it will be clear enough from its name. To add a new MIB to your SNMP tools, you have to obtain it from the vendor of your device and then install it on your system. Vendors usually make their MIBs freely available, so you shouldn't have any problems finding them.

Here are some of the major vendors of MIB sources, compiled at the time of writing:

| Vendor | MIBs |
| --- | --- |
| Cisco | http://www.cisco.com/public/sw-center/netmgmt/cmtk/mibs.shtml |
| Juniper | http://www.juniper.net/techpubs/software/index_mibs.html |
| Barracuda networks | https://techlib.barracuda.com/search/go/global?q=MIB |

A very useful resource is OIDView's free MIB database that you can find here:

http://www.oidview.com/mibs/detail.html

At the time of writing this, the database had more than 7,000 MIBs, so chances are you'll be able to find a MIB for the most obscure network device you might have to monitor.

MIBs are plain text files, so if you have a compressed archive, you will need to unpack it before you can install its contents. Once you have the plain text MIBS, it's a simple matter of copying them into /usr/share/snmp/mibs and then using the -m option to the SNMP commands to specify which MIB you want to load in addition to the default ones.

Should your MIBs collection become too big and you wanted to organize them in different directories, then you'll need to tell your tools where to find them. You have two options: either specify from the command line the directories you want your command to search for MIBs, or put this information in a configuration file so that your commands always know the MIBs' location. The options are discussed as follows:

- The first option is useful if you're just trying out a new MIB and seeing whether that's the one you need. Every Net-SNMP-based command will take a -m option that you can use to specify a specific MIB to load from the mibs directory. Here's a command for example:

```
$snmpwalk -m +CISCO-STUN-MIB -v 3  -u zabbix -a SHA -A zbxpassword
-l AuthPriv -x AES -X privpassword 10.10.1.9
```

This command will use SNMPv3 to contact the SNMP agent at 10.10.1.9 with the specified credentials and will load the CISCO-STUN-MIB that it will find in the /usr/share/snmp/mibs directory, in addition to those already loaded as default.

- The second option is more permanent and involves editing (or creating, if it's not already there) the /etc/snmp/snmp.conf file. Just add a line with the list of directories to search for mibs and another line that specifies which MIBs the commands should actually load (in this case, we'll load all of them), as follows:

```
mibdirs /usr/share/snmp/mibs:/usr/share/snmp/mibs/cisco:/usr/
share/snmp/mibs/juniper:/mnt/remote/shared_mibs/
mibs +ALL
```

As you can see, even if you keep your subdirectories in /usr/share/snmp/mibs, you'll have to specify each one you want automatically included. Once you have your MIBs installed and loaded, you'll be ready to fully explore your devices' SNMP agents. To perform a complete snmpwalk on a device can take quite a lot of time and produce a lot of output depending on how many OIDs it exposes. A router can have thousands of them, so it's advisable to redirect the command's output to a file so that you are able to reference it and explore it at any time you want without having to perform a complete walk on the device itself, as follows:

```
$snmpwalk -v 3  -u zabbix -a SHA -A zbxpassword -l AuthPriv -x AES -X
privpassword 10.10.1.9 > router-R1-snmp_baseline.txt
```

Another advantage of having the MIBs you need is that it'll be easier to create new SNMP items in Zabbix as you'll be able to specify the string version of an OID and not only its numerical value. Zabbix relies on the Net-SNMP library, so it will also reference any MIBs installed in your system's default directories.

So let's see how you can use the output of snmpwalk to create new Zabbix items.

# Mapping SNMP OIDs to Zabbix items

An SNMP value is composed of three different parts: the OID, the data type, and the value itself. When you use `snmpwalk` or `snmpget` to get values from an SNMP agent, the output looks like this:

```
SNMPv2-MIB::sysObjectID.0 = OID: CISCO-PRODUCTS-MIB::cisco3640

DISMAN-EVENT-MIB::sysUpTimeInstance = Timeticks: (83414) 0:13:54.14

SNMPv2-MIB::sysContact.0 = STRING:

SNMPv2-MIB::sysName.0 = STRING: R1

SNMPv2-MIB::sysLocation.0 = STRING: Upper floor room 13

SNMPv2-MIB::sysServices.0 = INTEGER: 78

SNMPv2-MIB::sysORLastChange.0 = Timeticks: (0) 0:00:00.00

...

IF-MIB::ifPhysAddress.24 = STRING: c4:1:22:4:f2:f

IF-MIB::ifPhysAddress.26 = STRING:

IF-MIB::ifPhysAddress.27 = STRING: c4:1:1e:c8:0:0

IF-MIB::ifAdminStatus.1 = INTEGER: up(1)

IF-MIB::ifAdminStatus.2 = INTEGER: down(2)

...
```

And so on.

The first part, the one before the = sign is, naturally, the OID. This will go into the SNMP OID field in the Zabbix item creation page and is the unique identifier for the metric you are interested in. Some OIDs represent a single and unique metric for the device, so they are easy to identify and address. In the above excerpt, one such OID is `DISMAN-EVENT-MIB::sysUpTimeInstance`. If you are interested in monitoring that OID, you'd only have to fill out the item creation form with the OID itself and then define an item name, a data type, and a retention policy, and you are ready to start monitoring it. In the case of an uptime value, time-ticks are expressed in seconds, so you'll choose a numeric decimal data type. We'll see in the next section how to choose Zabbix item data types and how to store values based on SNMP data types. You'll also want to store the value as is and optionally specify a unit of measure. This is because an uptime is already a relative value as it expresses the time elapsed since a device's latest boot. There would be no point in calculating a further delta when getting this measurement. Finally, you'll define a polling interval and choose a retention policy. In the following example, the polling interval is shown to be 5 minutes (300 seconds), the history retention policy as 3 days, and the trend storage period as one year. These should be sensible values as you don't normally need to store the detailed history of a value that either resets to zero, or, by definition, grows linearly by one tick every second.

The following screenshot encapsulates what has been discussed in this paragraph:

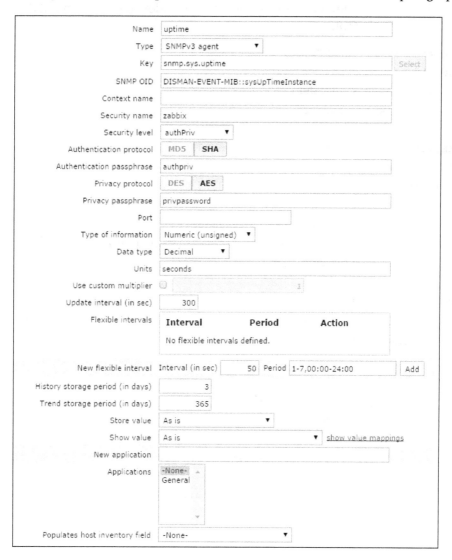

Remember that the item's key value still has to be unique at the host/template level as it will be referenced to by all other Zabbix components, from calculated items to triggers, maps, screens, and so on. Don't forget to put the right credentials for SNMPv3 if you are using this version of the protocol.

Many of the more interesting OIDs, though, are a bit more complex: multiple OIDs can be related to one another by means of the same index. Let's look at another `snmpwalk` output excerpt:

```
IF-MIB::ifNumber.0 = INTEGER: 26
IF-MIB::ifIndex.1 = INTEGER: 1
IF-MIB::ifIndex.2 = INTEGER: 2
IF-MIB::ifIndex.3 = INTEGER: 3
...
IF-MIB::ifDescr.1 = STRING: FastEthernet0/0
IF-MIB::ifDescr.2 = STRING: Serial0/0
IF-MIB::ifDescr.3 = STRING: FastEthernet0/1
...
IF-MIB::ifType.1 = INTEGER: ethernetCsmacd(6)
IF-MIB::ifType.2 = INTEGER: propPointToPointSerial(22)
IF-MIB::ifType.3 = INTEGER: ethernetCsmacd(6)
...
IF-MIB::ifMtu.1 = INTEGER: 1500
IF-MIB::ifMtu.2 = INTEGER: 1500
IF-MIB::ifMtu.3 = INTEGER: 1500
...
IF-MIB::ifSpeed.1 = Gauge32: 10000000
IF-MIB::ifSpeed.2 = Gauge32: 1544000
IF-MIB::ifSpeed.3 = Gauge32: 10000000
...
IF-MIB::ifPhysAddress.1 = STRING: c4:1:1e:c8:0:0
IF-MIB::ifPhysAddress.2 = STRING:
IF-MIB::ifPhysAddress.3 = STRING: c4:1:1e:c8:0:1
...
IF-MIB::ifAdminStatus.1 = INTEGER: up(1)
IF-MIB::ifAdminStatus.2 = INTEGER: down(2)
IF-MIB::ifAdminStatus.3 = INTEGER: down(2)
...
IF-MIB::ifOperStatus.1 = INTEGER: up(1)
IF-MIB::ifOperStatus.2 = INTEGER: down(2)
IF-MIB::ifOperStatus.3 = INTEGER: down(2)
...
IF-MIB::ifLastChange.1 = Timeticks: (1738) 0:00:17.38
```

```
IF-MIB::ifLastChange.2 = Timeticks: (1696) 0:00:16.96
IF-MIB::ifLastChange.3 = Timeticks: (1559) 0:00:15.59
...
IF-MIB::ifInOctets.1 = Counter32: 305255
IF-MIB::ifInOctets.2 = Counter32: 0
IF-MIB::ifInOctets.3 = Counter32: 0
...
IF-MIB::ifInDiscards.1 = Counter32: 0
IF-MIB::ifInDiscards.2 = Counter32: 0
IF-MIB::ifInDiscards.3 = Counter32: 0
...
IF-MIB::ifInErrors.1 = Counter32: 0
IF-MIB::ifInErrors.2 = Counter32: 0
IF-MIB::ifInErrors.3 = Counter32: 0
...
IF-MIB::ifOutOctets.1 = Counter32: 347968
IF-MIB::ifOutOctets.2 = Counter32: 0
IF-MIB::ifOutOctets.3 = Counter32: 0
```

As you can see, for every network interface, there are several OIDs, each one detailing a specific aspect of the interface: its name, its type, whether it's up or down, the amount of traffic coming in or going out, and so on. The different OIDs are related through their last number, the actual index of the OID. Looking at the preceding excerpt, we know that the device has 26 interfaces, of which we are showing some values for just the first three. By correlating the index numbers, we also know that interface 1 is called FastEthernet0/0, its MAC address is c4:1:1e:c8:0:0, the interface is up and has been up for just 17 seconds, and some traffic already went through it.

Now, one way to monitor several of these metrics for the same interface is to manually correlate these values when creating the items, putting the complete OID in the SNMP OID field, and making sure that both the item key and its name reflect the right interface. This process is not only prone to errors during the setup phase, but it could also introduce some inconsistencies down the road. There is no guarantee, in fact, that the index will remain consistent across hardware or software upgrades or even across configurations when it comes to more volatile states like the number of VLANs or routing tables instead of network interfaces. Fortunately Zabbix provides a feature, called **dynamic indexes**, that allows you to actually correlate different OIDs in the same SNMP OID field so that you can define an index based on the index exposed by another OID.

This means that if you want to know the admin status of `FastEthernet0/0`, you don't need to find the index associated with `FastEthernet0/0` (in this case it would be 1) and then add that index to `IF-MIB::ifAdminStatus` of the base OID, hoping that it won't ever change in the future. You can instead use the following code:

```
IF-MIB::ifAdminStatus["index", "IF-MIB::ifDescr",
  "FastEthernet0/0"]
```

Upon using the preceding code in the SNMP OID field of your item, the item will dynamically find the index of the `IF-MIB::ifDescr` OID where the value is `FastEthernet0/0` and append it to `IF-MIB::ifAdminStatus` in order to get the right status for the right interface.

If you organize your items this way, you'll always be sure that related items actually show the right related values for the component you are interested in and not those of another one because things changed on the device's side without your knowledge. Moreover, we'll build on this technique to develop low-level discovery of a device as we'll see in *Chapter 4, Discovering Your Network*.

You can use the same technique to get other interesting information out of a device. Consider, for example, the following excerpt:

```
ENTITY-MIB::entPhysicalVendorType.1 = OID: CISCO-ENTITY-VENDORTYPE-
OID-MIB::cevChassis3640
ENTITY-MIB::entPhysicalVendorType.2 = OID: CISCO-ENTITY-VENDORTYPE-
OID-MIB::cevContainerSlot
ENTITY-MIB::entPhysicalVendorType.3 = OID: CISCO-ENTITY-VENDORTYPE-
OID-MIB::cevCpu37452fe

ENTITY-MIB::entPhysicalClass.1 = INTEGER: chassis(3)
ENTITY-MIB::entPhysicalClass.2 = INTEGER: container(5)
ENTITY-MIB::entPhysicalClass.3 = INTEGER: module(9)

ENTITY-MIB::entPhysicalName.1 = STRING: 3745 chassis
ENTITY-MIB::entPhysicalName.2 = STRING: 3640 Chassis Slot 0
ENTITY-MIB::entPhysicalName.3 = STRING: c3745 Motherboard with Fast
Ethernet on Slot 0

ENTITY-MIB::entPhysicalHardwareRev.1 = STRING: 2.0
ENTITY-MIB::entPhysicalHardwareRev.2 = STRING:
ENTITY-MIB::entPhysicalHardwareRev.3 = STRING: 2.0

ENTITY-MIB::entPhysicalSerialNum.1 = STRING: FTX0945W0MY
ENTITY-MIB::entPhysicalSerialNum.2 = STRING:
ENTITY-MIB::entPhysicalSerialNum.3 = STRING: XXXXXXXXXX
```

It should be immediately clear to you that you can find the chassis's serial number by creating an item with:

```
ENTITY-MIB::entPhysicalSerialNum["index", "ENTITY-
MIB::entPhysicalName", "3745 chassis"]
```

Then you can specify, in the same item, that it should populate the `Serial Number` field of the host's inventory. This is how you can have a more automatic, dynamic population of inventory fields.

The possibilities are endless as we've only just scratched the surface of what any given device can expose as SNMP metrics. Before you go and find your favorite OIDs to monitor though, let's have a closer look at the preceding examples, and let's discuss data types.

# Getting data types right

We have already seen how an OID's value has a specific data type that is usually clearly stated with the default `snmpwalk` command. In the preceding examples, you can clearly see the data type just after the = sign, before the actual value. There are a number of SNMP data types—some still current and some deprecated. You can find the official list and documentation in RFC2578 (`http://tools.ietf.org/html/rfc2578`), but let's have a look at the most important ones from the perspective of a Zabbix user:

| SNMP type | Description | Suggested Zabbix item type and options |
|---|---|---|
| INTEGER | This can have negative values and is usually used for enumerations | • Numeric unsigned, decimal<br>• Store value as is<br>• Show with value mappings |
| STRING | This is a regular character string and can contain new lines | • Text<br>• Store value as is |
| OID | This is an SNMP object identifier | • Character<br>• Store value as is |
| IpAddress | IPv4 only | • Character<br>• Store value as is |

| SNMP type | Description | Suggested Zabbix item type and options |
|---|---|---|
| Counter32 | This includes only non-negative and nondecreasing values | • Numeric unsigned, decimal<br>• Store value as delta (speed per second) |
| Gauge32 | This includes only non-negative values, which can decrease | • Numeric unsigned, decimal<br>• Store value as is |
| Counter64 | This includes non-negative and nondecreasing 64-bit values | • Numeric unsigned, decimal<br>• Store value as delta (speed per second) |
| TimeTicks | This includes non-negative, nondecreasing values | • Numeric unsigned, decimal<br>• Store value as is |

First of all, remember that the above suggestions are just that—suggestions. You should always evaluate how to store your data on a case-by-case basis, but you'll probably find that in many cases those are indeed the most useful settings.

Moving on to the actual data types, remember that the command line SNMP tools by default parse the values and show some already interpreted information. This is especially true for `Timeticks` values and for `INTEGER` values when these are used as enumerations. In other words, you see the following from the command line:

```
VRRP-MIB::vrrpNotificationCntl.0 = INTEGER: disabled(2)
```

However, what is actually passed as a request is the bare OID:

```
1.3.6.1.2.1.68.1.2.0
```

The SNMP agent will respond with just the value, which, in this case, is the value 2.

This means that in the case of enumerations, Zabbix will just receive and store a number and not the string `disabled(2)` as seen from the command line. If you want to display monitoring values that are a bit clearer, you can apply value mappings to your numeric items. **Value maps** contain the mapping between numeric values and arbitrary string representations for a human-friendly representation. You can specify which one you need in the item configuration form, as follows:

| | | | |
|---|---|---|---|
| Authentication protocol | **As is** | | |
| Authentication passphrase | APC Battery Replacement Status | | |
| Privacy protocol | APC Battery Status | | |
| Privacy passphrase | Dell Open Manage System Status | | |
| Port | | | |
| Type of information | Host status | | |
| Data type | HP Insight System Status | | |
| Units | Maintenance status | | |
| Use custom multiplier | Service state | | |
| Update interval (in sec) | SNMP device status (hrDeviceStatus) | | |
| Flexible intervals | SNMP interface status (ifAdminStatus) | **Action** | |
| | SNMP interface status (ifOperStatus) | | |
| New flexible interval | VMware status | 00-24:00 | Add |
| History storage period (in days) | VMware VirtualMachinePowerState | | |
| Trend storage period (in days) | Windows service state | | |
| Store value | Zabbix agent ping status | | |
| Show value | As is ▼ | show value mappings | |

Zabbix comes with a few predefined value mappings. You can create your own mappings by following the **show value mappings** link and, provided you have admin roles on Zabbix, you'll be taken to a page where you can configure all value mappings that will be used by Zabbix. From there, click on **Create value map** in the upper-right corner of the page, and you'll be able to create a new mapping. Not all INTEGER values are enumerations, but those that are used as such will be clearly recognizable from your command-line tools as they will be defined as INTEGER values but will show a string label along with the actual value, just as in the preceding example.

On the other hand, when they are not used as enumerations, they can represent different things depending on the context. As seen in the previous paragraph, they can represent the number of indexes available for a given OID. They can also represent application or protocol-specific values, such as default MTU, default TTL, route metrics, and so on.

The main difference between gauges, counters, and integers is that integers can assume negative values, while gauges and counters cannot. In addition to that, counters can only increase or wrap around and start again from the bottom of their value range once they reach the upper limits of it. From the perspective of Zabbix, this marks the difference in how you'll want to store their values.

Gauges are usually employed when a value can vary within a given range, such as the speed of an interface, the amount of free memory, or any limits and timeouts you might find for notifications, the number of instances, and so on. In all of these cases, the value can increase or decrease in time, so you'll want to store them as they are because once put on a graph, they'll draw a meaningful curve.

Counters, on the other hand, can only increase by definition. They are typically used to show how many packets were processed by an interface, how many were dropped, how many errors were encountered, and so on. If you store counter values as they are, you'll find in your graphs some ever-ascending curves that won't tell you very much for your monitoring or capacity planning purposes. This is why you'll usually want to track a counter's amount of change in time, more than its actual value. To do that, Zabbix offers two different ways to store deltas or differences between successive values.

The delta (simple change) storage method does exactly what it says: it simply computes the difference between the currently received value and the previously received one, and stores the result. It doesn't take into consideration the elapsed time between the two measurements, nor the fact that the result can even have a negative value if the counter overflows. The fact is that most of the time, you'll be very interested in evaluating how much time has passed between two different measurements and in treating correctly any negative values that can appear as a result.

The delta (speed per second) will divide the difference between the currently received value and the previously received one by the difference between the current timestamp and the previous one, as follows:

```
(value - prev_value)/(time - prev_time)
```

This will ensure that the scale of the change will always be constant, as opposed to the scale of the simple change delta, which will vary every time you modify the update interval of the item, giving you inconsistent results. Moreover, the speed-per-second delta will ignore any negative values and just wait for the next measurement, so you won't find any false dips in your graph due to overflowing.

Finally, while SNMP uses specific data types for IP addresses and SNMP OIDs, there are no such types in Zabbix, so you'll need to map them to some kind of string item. The suggested type here is character as both values won't be bigger than 255 characters and won't contain any newlines.

String values, on the other hand, can be quite long as the SNMP specification allows for 65,535-character-long texts; however, text that long would be of little practical value. Even if they are usually much shorter, string values can often contain newlines and be longer than 255 characters.

Consider, for example, the following `SysDescr` OID for this device:

```
NMPv2-MIB::sysDescr.0 = STRING: Cisco IOS Software, 3700 Software
(C3745-ADVENTERPRISEK9_SNA-M), Version 12.4(15)T14, RELEASE SOFTWARE
(fc2)^M
Technical Support: http://www.cisco.com/techsupport^M
Copyright (c) 1986-2010 by Cisco Systems, Inc.^M
Compiled Tue 17-Aug-10 12:56 by prod_rel_tea
```

As you can see, the string spans multiple lines, and it's definitely longer than 255 characters. This is why the suggested type for string values is `text` as it allows text of arbitrary length and structure. On the other hand, if you're sure that a specific OID value will always be much shorter and simpler, you can certainly use the `character` data type for your corresponding Zabbix item.

Now, you are truly ready to get the most out of your devices' SNMP agents as you are now able to find the OID you want to monitor and map them perfectly to Zabbix items, down to how to store the values, their data types, with what frequency, and with any value mapping that might be necessary.

It's now time to explore the other aspect of SNMP: traps.

# SNMP traps

SNMP traps are a bit of an oddball when compared to all the other Zabbix item types. Unlike other items, SNMP traps do not report a simple measurement, but an event of some type. In other words, they are the result of some kind of check or computation made by the SNMP agent and sent over to the monitoring server as a status report. An SNMP trap can be issued every time a host is rebooted, an interface is down, a disk is damaged, or a UPS has lost power and is keeping servers up using its battery.

This kind of information contrasts with Zabbix's basic assumption that an item is a simple metric not directly related to a specific event. On the other hand, there's no other way to be aware of certain situations if not through an SNMP trap either because there are no related metrics (consider, for example, the event *the server is being shut down*) or because the appliance's only way to convey its status is through a bunch of SNMP objects and traps.

So traps are of relatively limited use to Zabbix as you can't do much more than build a simple trigger out of every trap and then notify about the event (not much point in graphing a trap or building calculated items on it). Nevertheless, they might prove essential for a complete monitoring solution.

To manage SNMP traps effectively, Zabbix needs a couple of helper tools: the snmptrapd daemon to actually handle connections from the SNMP agents and some kind of script to correctly format every trap and pass it to the Zabbix server for further processing.

# Snmptrapd

If you have compiled SNMP support into the Zabbix server, you should already have the complete SNMP suite installed, which contains the SNMP daemon and the SNMP trap daemon along with the utilities we have used in the previous section.

Just as the Zabbix server has a bunch of daemon processes that listen on TCP port 10051 for incoming connections (from agents, proxies, and nodes), snmptrapd is the daemon process that listens on UDP port 162 for incoming traps coming from remote SNMP agents.

Once installed, snmptrapd reads its configuration options from an snmptrapd. conf file that can be usually found in the /etc/snmp/ directory. The bare minimum configuration for snmptrapd requires the definition of a user and a privacy level for SNMP v3, as follows:

```
createUser zbxuser SHA auth AES priv
authUser log,execute,net zbxuser
```

The above configuration will enable snmptrapd to receive SNMPv3 INFORM packets. These are just like regular SNMP traps, with two differences: the first one is that while an agent won't expect a response after sending a trap, INFORM packets are acknowledged, so snmptrapd will send a response for every trap received. But the most important difference is that with INFORM packets, the authoritative EngineID will be that of the receiving party and not the sending party as with regular traps. This means that you'll have to specify your server's EngineID to every device that will send SNMPv3 INFORM packets. Since you'll have to configure them to send packets to the server anyway, this won't mean too much work. Many agents automatically discover a peer's EngineID before sending an INFORM, but if you need to set it yourself, you can discover your server's EngineID using snmpget and asking for the snmpEngineID.0 OID.

If you want to use regular SNMP traps, you'll have to insert a new createUser line for every agent that will send traps to the server, with each one specifying the correct EngineID of the agent sending traps.

With this minimal configuration, `snmptrapd` will limit itself to log the trap to `syslog`. While it could be possible to extract this information and send it to Zabbix, it's easier to tell `snmptrapd` how it should handle traps. While the daemon has no processing capabilities of its own, it can execute any command or application either using the `trapHandle` directive, or leveraging its embedded Perl functionality. The latter is more efficient as the daemon won't have to fork a new process and wait for its execution to finish, so it's the recommended one if you plan to receive a significant number of traps. Just add the following line to `snmptrapd.conf`:

```
perl do "/usr/local/bin/zabbix_trap_receiver.pl";
```

> You can get the `zabbix_trap_receiver` script from the Zabbix sources. It's located in `misc/snmptrap/zabbix_trap_receiver.pl`.
>
> Be sure to check that you also have the Net-SNMP Perl module installed. If you need it, a simple `yum install net-snmp-perl` command should take care of everything.

Once restarted, the `snmptrapd` daemon will execute the Perl script you specified to process every trap received, translating it into a format that can be easily parsed by the Zabbix server. In the following section, we'll see how an SNMP trap is translated and used by Zabbix.

# Transforming a trap into a Zabbix item

The Perl script included in the Zabbix distribution works as a translator from an SNMP trap format to a Zabbix item measurement. For every trap received, it will format it according to the rules defined in the script and will output the result in a log file. By default, the log file is called `/tmp/zabbix_traps.tmp`. You need to make sure that the same file is read by Zabbix by setting the following parameters in `/etc/zabbix/zabbix_server.conf`:

```
### Option: StartSNMPTrapper
#           If 1, SNMP trapper process is started.
#
# Mandatory: no
# Range: 0-1
# Default:
StartSNMPTrapper=1

### Option: SNMPTrapperFile
#           Temporary file used for passing data from SNMP trap daemon to
the server.
```

```
#        Must be the same as in zabbix_trap_receiver.pl or SNMPTT
configuration file.
SNMPTrapperFile=/tmp/zabbix_traps.tmp
```

The log file will have a format similar to the following example:

```
03:47:10 2014/12/09 ZBXTRAP 127.0.0.1
PDU INFO:
  notificationtype              TRAP
  version                       0
  receivedfrom                  UDP: [127.0.0.1]:34373->[127.0.0.1]
  errorstatus                   0
  messageid                     0
  community                     public
  transactionid                 3
  errorindex                    0
  requestid                     0
VARBINDS:
  DISMAN-EVENT-MIB::sysUpTimeInstance type=67 value=Timeticks: (55)
0:00:00.55
    SNMPv2-MIB::snmpTrapOID.0      type=6  value=OID: IF-
MIB::linkDown.0.33
    IF-MIB::linkDown              type=4  value=Hex-STRING: E2 80 9C 54
45 53 54 4D 45 4E 4F 57 E2 80 9D
    SNMP-COMMUNITY-MIB::snmpTrapCommunity.0 type=4  value=STRING:
"public"
    SNMPv2-MIB::snmpTrapEnterprise.0 type=6  value=OID: IF-MIB::linkDown
```

The ZBXTRAP followed by the IP address will mark the start of a new log stanza. The rest of the log will contain all details about the trap, so you'll be able to act on any of those.

The Zabbix server will in turn monitor the aforesaid log file and process every new line as an SNMP trap item, basically matching the content of the log to any trap item defined for the relevant host.

As you've already seen, the first part of the log line is used by the Zabbix trap receiver to match a trap with its corresponding host. The rest is matched to the aforesaid host's SNMP trap item's `regexp` definitions and its content added to every matching item's history of values. This means that if you wish to have a `linkDown` trap item for a given host, you'll need to configure an SNMP trap item with an `snmptrap["linkDown"]` key, as follows:

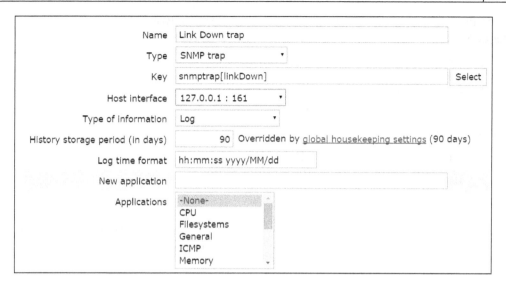

You might need to make sure that the log time format you specify in the item's configuration will match the one used by the Perl script. You'll also have to check that the host's interface will match the one logged by snmptrapd because it's the one piece of data Zabbix will use to match traps to hosts.

From now on, you'll be able to see the contents of the trap in the item's data history.

Moving on from SNMP, there are still other data sources that you can rely on to get monitoring data into Zabbix: for the purposes of this book, the most interesting ones are log files. Compared to SNMP, they can be tricky to work with, but they do have their uses, so let's explore them for a while.

# Getting netflow from the devices to the monitoring server

Netflow is a protocol originally developed by Cisco to collect and monitor statistics of network traffic on a device. After the initial release, many vendors started providing their own implementation of the protocol. In 2008 IETF standardized netflow and published **Internet Protocol Flow Information eXport (IPFIX)** based on netflow v9 with some extensions. However, *netflow* somehow remains the existing name of the protocol in fact but not necessarily by legal right, so that's the one we'll use here.

A netflow record contains information about a single network flow. A flow is a sequence of packets that share some common properties:

- IP protocol
- Source IP address
- Source port (for TCP and UDP)
- Destination IP address
- Destination port (for TCP and UDP)
- Input interface
- Type of service

For each flow, a record exposes many different values, which change with netflow versions and implementations. Here are the most common ones:

- Input interface of the device
- Output interface of the device
- Flow start time
- Flow end time
- Number of bytes in the flow
- Number of packets in the flow
- Source IP address
- Source IP port
- Source IP mask
- Destination IP address
- Destination IP port
- Destination IP mask
- ICMP type and code
- TCP flags
- IP address of the immediate next-hop

It should be immediately clear to you that this type of information can be extremely useful to a network administrator as it allows you to build a picture of all the traffic traversing your network. It can also be used to identify anomalous traffic and traffic to and from IP addresses or ports that should not be there, or as forensic evidence after an incident. Moreover, it can be used as a source for capacity-planning analysis to identify bottlenecks in your network, periods of peak use, and top talkers among your servers and devices.

Finally, as we were explaining previously, it's a good candidate for a Zabbix log item as flow data is useful even if it is not directly related to the host that generated it (even if it's still useful to track that piece of information whenever possible).

So, let's see how to get netflow data into Zabbix.

First of all, you'll have to configure your device to send flow data to a server. In the case of a Cisco device, here are the configuration commands that you need to issue (remember to substitute all references to the example Zabbix server with the real ones that apply to your environment):

```
R1(config)#ip flow-export destination 192.168.234.131 9995
R1(config)#ip flow-export version 9
R1(config)#interface f0/0
R1(config-if)#ip flow ingress
R1(config-if)#ip flow egress
R1(config-if)#exit
```

In the first line, we specify the IP address of our Zabbix server and the UDP port the device should send netflow information to.

The second line sets the netflow version.

In the third line, we go into interface f0/0 mode. Please note that you'll have to explicitly enable netflow for every interface you are interested in. This is usually not a problem because if you configure netflow on the right interfaces of your routers, you'll see most, if not all of your traffic anyway: you won't need to enable netflow on every interface of every network device you have.

The fourth line enables netflow monitoring for incoming traffic on interface f0/0, while the fifth line enables netflow monitoring for outgoing traffic on the same interface. If you want to enable netflow on other interfaces, you'll need to repeat lines 3 to 5 for every interface you are interested in.

Repeat the whole process for all the routers you want to get flow information from, and once you are done, you are ready to turn to your Zabbix server.

# Receiving netflow data on your server

To actually receive and process netflow packets on a server, you need a daemon that will listen on a specified UDP port, and that will understand the netflow protocol. On Linux, such daemons and associated tools are contained in the nfdump package.

**Nfdump** is a collection of tools that will enable you to capture netflow data, store it on disk, filter it, and analyze it. The most important components are:

- `nfcapd`: This is the daemon component that listens for incoming netflow data and stores it on disk in binary format
- `nfdump`: This is similar to `tcpdump`; it reads and filters `nfcapd` files, and outputs readable data

So the basic dataflow will be similar to this one:

1. A router sends netflow data to the server.
2. On the server, `nfcapd` captures the data and stores it in binary files.
3. A scheduled `nfdump` process will read the binary files and populate a human readable log with netflow information.
4. A Zabbix agent will read the log and send data to the Zabbix server according to the item's configuration.

We have already taken care of point 1, so let's see how to install and configure the `nfdump` package, before looking into the Zabbix side.

Unfortunately, there are no readymade `rpm` packets for `nfdump`, so we'll need to find the source code, compile it, and install it. This is usually a straightforward process. First of all, let's install some required dependencies for `nfdump`:

```
# yum install rrdtool rrdtool-devel rrdtool-doc perl-rrdtool
```

Then, we'll need to download the latest sources. At the moment of writing this, the latest available version is 1.6.12. You can download the package from `http://sourceforge.net/projects/nfdump/` and then transfer it to your server. Once you have `tar.gz` ready, unpack it:

```
$ tar xvzf nfdump-1.6.12.tar.gz
```

Then move into the `nfdump-1.6.12` directory and run the usual configure, make, and make install sequence. If you want to install `nfdump` in the main directories instead of the `/usr/local` tree, just pass the `-prefix` option to the configure script. In the following example, that's what we'll use:

```
$ cd nfdump-1.6.12
$ ./configure -prefix=/usr --sysconfdir=/etc
$ make
$ su root
# make install
```

Once installed, you can add a dedicated user for `nfcapd` so that it doesn't have to run as root and set a working directory for it:

```
# useradd -s /sbin/nologin netflow
# mkdir -p /var/nfdump/nfcapd
# mkdir -p /var/nfdump/logs
# chown -R netflow /var/nfdump
```

When you run `nfcapd`, it will create its binary files under /var/nfdump/nfcapd. Nfcapd files are rotated, by default, once every five minutes and can be separated into one dump collection (current and rotated files) per sending host or a single collection for all sending hosts. They can also be expired after a set amount of time. You are now ready to wait for netflow data and transform it into a log file. To do that, you'll need to pass the right option to `nfcapd`. Since there are quite a few options to pass, let's build the command line little by little. Please don't run the intermediate commands, but only the final one; `nfcapd` will complain about missing options and refuse to run.

First of all, we'll pass some options that will instruct `nfcapd` to go into daemon mode (-D), to compress output (-z), to run as user netflow (-u), and to listen on port 9995 (-p):

```
# nfcapd -D -z -u netflow -p 9995
```

Then, we'll need to add some options about data sources. The accepted current method is to use the -n switch. We'll also instruct `nfcapd` to create additional subdirectories to store the cap files to better organize them (-S):

```
# nfcapd -D -z -u netflow -p 9995 -n R1,192.168.11.9,/var/nfdump/nfcapd
-n R2,10.10.1.254,/var/nfdump/nfcapd -S2
```

As you can see, you'll have to specify a different -n option for every source you configure. If you have many netflow sources, it might be better to run different instances of `nfcapd` on different UDP ports so as to share the load between different processes. In that case, just remember to configure your devices accordingly so that they send their traffic to the correct UDP port. The -S2 option will create additional year/month/day/hour directories under /var/nfdump/nfcapd to store current and rotated files.

Nfcapd files are rotated every five minutes, and if your network has a lot of traffic, your nfcapd directory can become huge. You could schedule a separate job to clean them up, but with the -e option, nfcapd will be able to also take care of that. Just set the expiration parameter with nfexpire and nfcapd will pick them up:

```
# nfexpire -u /var/nfdump/nfcapd -s 15G -t 90d
# nfcapd -D -z -u netflow -p 9995 -n R1,192.168.11.9,/var/nfdump/nfcapd
-n R2,10.10.1.254,/var/nfdump/nfcapd -S2 -e
```

In the above example, we set the size limit of the directory to 15 gigabytes, and the cap (maximum) file age to 90 days. Files will be deleted by nfcapd whenever one of these limits is reached. The last line in the preceding command now contains all the parameters we need for basic netflow dumping. If you run it (don't forget the nfexpire command too) or put it into a startup script, nfcapd will listen on the specified network port for incoming netflow data and write it to the directories you specified.

Once you have some data in, you can read it with nfdump and output a human-readable set of records:

```
$ nfdump -r /var/nfdump/nfcapd/2014/10/29/02/nfcapd.201410290250 -o
extended
Date flow start          Duration Proto      Src IP Addr:Port          Dst IP
Addr:Port    Flags Tos  Packets     Bytes        pps       bps      Bpp Flows

2014-10-29 02:51:53.160    63.545 TCP     10.13.27.151:80      ->
123.43.98.124:6523  .AP.SF   0        128       8412          0         550
56    1
2014-10-29 02:53:13.370    23.135 TCP     64.76.73.121:25      ->
10.138.41.151:7643   .AP.SF   0        51 2450                0         551      56
1
...
Time window: Oct 29 2014 02:50:00 - Oct 29 2014 02:54:56
```

This is getting closer to our objective. If you run nfdump and redirect its output to a file instead of the screen, there you have the log file we've been talking about in the last several pages. To do that, you are probably thinking of setting up a cron job that will find the latest nfcapd files that weren't already parsed by nfdump, make nfdump read them while specifying a time window so that your log file won't contain duplicated data, and add the aforesaid output to a log file that will be monitored by Zabbix. This can be a nontrivial exercise when you consider that nfcapd will continually produce new files and will put them in new directories all the time. Moreover, you'll need to keep some kind of execution state with the timestamp of the last time nfdump was run in order to avoid the aforesaid duplicates.

It turns out that you'll be able to avoid all this work, thanks to a nice option for nfcapd, the -x option. So let's rewrite the nfcapd command one last time:

```
# nfcapd -D -z -u netflow -p 9995 -n R1,192.168.11.9,/var/nfdump/nfcapd
-n R2,10.10.1.254,/var/nfdump/nfcapd -S2 -e -x 'nfdump -q -o extended -r
%d/%f >> /var/nfdump/logs/zabbix_netflow.log'
```

The -x command executes an arbitrary command every time a dump file is rotated.
You can reference the dump file and the base directory with the %d/%f macros. This
means that nfdump will always be executed on new data and only once per dump
file. Suddenly, you won't need to schedule any complicated cron job to generate the
final, human-readable netflow log file. We also added a -q option to suppress the
header and statistics printing to keep the log file clean.

 You might still want to configure some log rotation for the /var/
nfdump/logs/zabbix_netflow.log file. If you let it grow
unchecked, it will fill up your disk space in due time!

It's finally time to make Zabbix aware of the netflow log file.

# Monitoring a log file with Zabbix

As already explained, log file monitoring needs a Zabbix agent. For illustration
purposes, we will assume that you have installed nfdump on the same box as the
Zabbix server, and that the log file is thus locally available. It goes without saying
that you could also install nfdump, along with a Zabbix agent, on a separated,
possibly dedicated machine. It won't make any difference from Zabbix's perspective.

Basic item creation is fairly straightforward, just point the item key to the correct file
path and you're good to go. Please note, in the following example, the timestamp
parsing field:

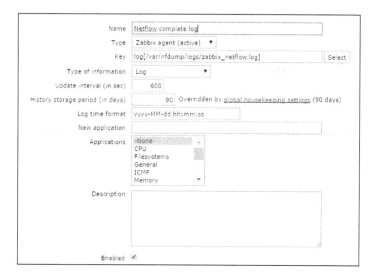

This is all you need for basic log file monitoring. For further explorations, the log key accepts different options, among which the most interesting are those related to regular expression filtering and output so that you can also create additional items that will only extract the exact information you need (for instance, bytes per second of a flow) and use it as raw data, just as you would use any other Zabbix item. Zabbix's own official documentation is excellent in this respect, so you are encouraged to find out more at `https://www.zabbix.com/documentation/2.4/manual/config/items/itemtypes/log_items`.

On the `nfdump` side, there are many more options and features available to `nfdump`, we've really only scratched the surface to keep things simple. We don't have the space to fully explore it here, but if you're willing to spend some time exploring the tool, you'll find that `nfdump` is not only capable of powerful traffic filtering, just as `tcpdump` is, but it can also create statistics and aggregated data on virtually every aspect of a flow, from network ports to packet sizes, and so on. Combine this with Zabbix's powerful external script items, and you can easily see that you can slice and dice your data; however, if you want, bring it into Zabbix for further processing, graphing, and alarming. Really, the sky is the limit when you learn to combine these tools together.

# Summary

In this chapter, you have learned the different possibilities Zabbix offers to the enterprising network administrator.

You should now be able to choose, design, and implement all the monitoring items you need, based on the methods illustrated in the preceding paragraphs: simple checks that are more useful and powerful than the name implies; the all-powerful SNMP protocol, both as get values and as traps; log files in general; and the infinitely useful netflow protocol

The next chapter will build on the information exposed in this chapter and will focus more on server monitoring and how to extract information from DNS servers, web servers, proxies, and other appliances. These are important, if often overlooked, components of a network even from the perspective of a network administrator, and you'll find many useful tips on how to monitor them.

# 3
# Monitoring Your Network Services

In every environment, especially in a large one, there are many network critical services that are directly tied on the network infrastructure. Many of them can be monitored by the system administrators, but the core critical services for the whole network are better if they are monitored directly by the network administrator.

Between those critical services, we can find the following:

- DNS
- DHCP
- NTP
- Apache proxy / reverse proxies
- Proxy cache Squid

As it is easy to understand, even if those services are provided from some dedicated server and not network devices, the metrics that you are acquiring from them are fundamental. Those metrics, indeed, play a critical role when you would like to set up a proactive alarm.

An example of a service that can cause a lot of confusion in your network can be the DNS, the DHCP, or even the NTP. In an ideal environment, all those services need to be responsive, and even the response time is crucial; if each one of those components becomes unresponsive, they will act as the weakest link of your infrastructure, causing a lot of problems that will be quickly propagated to the whole network. A simple NTP server can introduce confusion in the logs of your systems or even cause an issue in your connections. Working on a practical example, try to imagine that you have all your accounts stored in an LDAP. Well, if the LDAP takes too much time to resolve the UID/GID of your account, you can have issues propagated to all your systems. An unresponsive LDAP can cause filesystem issues and even NAS issues, and if all your accounts are stored there, even an *ls* can literally take ages, with a big impact on the whole infrastructure. Here, we are not considering the DNS, where a dysfunction can be even worse.

Also, those services need to be taken under surveillance as, if they become unresponsive, quite soon they will accumulate requests to serve, and if the environment is not ready, they will be flooded by their own queries in a queue, with a global impact on our infrastructure.

In this chapter, we will go through all the main services that a network admin should monitor to avoid these kinds of issues. Then, the reader will learn and understand the importance of an effective proactive alarm to avoid a quick escalation of issues across the network.

# Monitoring the DNS

The first network component we will analyze and see how to monitor is the DNS.

The most popular DNS server is BIND, which is also one of the oldest packages produced. Here, in the next example, we assume you have BIND 9.6 or later.

Starting with version 9.6, there is a brand new feature that is not even mentioned in the main page (of Red Hat Linux at least). This feature is a built-in web server that provides statistics about BIND in a very simple way thought HTTP. To enable this feature, it is enough to add those lines to your BIND9 configuration file, /etc/ named.conf:

```
statistics-channels {
   inet 127.0.0.1 port 8053 allow { 127.0.0.1; };
};
```

The line we have just added is a good example as the statistics' access is controlled and restricted to the localhost.

BIND, by default, will use the standard 80 HTTP port if you don't specify the port. Also please take care to limit the access to the statistic channel; to do so, you can use this clause:

```
allow {  address_match_list  }
```

If you don't specify the `allow` clause, BIND will accept connections from any address. This needs to be avoided.

Once this is done, all you have to do is restart your service with:

```
$ service named restart
Stopping named:                          [  OK  ]
Starting named:                          [  OK  ]
```

Now, you can even use `curl` to call your web server and have delivered to you all the statistics:

```
# curl http://127.0.0.1:8053
<?xml version="1.0" encoding="UTF-8"?>
<?xml-stylesheet type="text/xsl" href="/bind9.xsl"?>
<isc version="1.0">
  <bind>
    <statistics version="2.2">
      <views>
        <view>
          <name>_default</name>
          <zones>
....
        <summary>
          <TotalUse>5965501</TotalUse>
          <InUse>1502936</InUse>
          <BlockSize>4718592</BlockSize>
          <ContextSize>3595936</ContextSize>
          <Lost>0</Lost>
        </summary>
      </memory>
    </statistics>
  </bind>
</isc>
```

Now, we have two ways to retrieve the statistics:

- Configure BIND to write the statistics in the stat file (old method)
- Configure BIND to use the built-in HTTP web service

The first and old method can be used for servers that are not under a heavy load; the new method using the `statistics-channels` is on the other hand lightweight and very easy to manage. Nowadays this one is the preferred method to use.

 Starting from BIND 9.10, the statistics can be delivered in either the XML or the JSON format. The previous version of BIND offered only statistics on XML v2 or V3. Starting with BIND 9.10, the XML statistics are available only in V3 format. Anyway, the JSON format is significantly faster than XML and even lightweight to provide.

Now, to filter the output obtained by `curl`, there is an interesting utility that unfortunately is not a standard RPM distributed by Red Hat. The tool we are going to use on those examples is **xml2**.

This xml2 is an XML processing tool that can be used to parse and read the XML envelopes and rewrite them as a flat format. The flat format is really useful to be manipulated with shell scripts. Then, first of all, you need to download this utility (the source code is available at `http://download.ofb.net/gale/xml2-0.5.tar.gz`). Here's the output summary:

```
# wget http://download.ofb.net/gale/xml2-0.5.tar.gz
--2014-11-01 10:43:44--  http://download.ofb.net/gale/xml2-0.5.tar.gz
Resolving download.ofb.net... 64.13.131.34
Connecting to download.ofb.net|64.13.131.34|:80... connected.
HTTP request sent, awaiting response... 200 OK
Length: 86318 (84K) [application/x-gzip]
Saving to: "xml2-0.5.tar.gz"

100%[====================================>] 86,318        155K/s    in 0.5s

2014-11-01 10:43:45 (155 KB/s) - "xml2-0.5.tar.gz" saved [86318/86318]
```

Perform the following steps to obtain the results set out in the preceding paragraph:

1.  Explode the package, as follows:

    ```
    # tar -zxvf xml2-0.5.tar.gz
    xml2-0.5/
    xml2-0.5/configure.ac
    xml2-0.5/aclocal.m4
    ...
    xml2-0.5/csv2.c
    xml2-0.5/xml2.c
    ```

2. Step into the directory, as follows:

```
# cd xml2-0.5
```

3. Run the usual `./configure` followed by `make` and `make install`, as follows:

```
# ./configure && make
```

Then, as root, you can now run the following command:

```
#make install
```

Once all this has been completed, you are ready to run the utility.

To make you better understand what this tool exactly does, you can run the following command:

```
# curl http://localhost:8053/ 2>/dev/null | xml2 | grep -A1
queries
/isc/bind/statistics/server/queries-in/rdtype/name=A
/isc/bind/statistics/server/queries-in/rdtype/counter=11230
/isc/bind/statistics/server/queries-in/rdtype
/isc/bind/statistics/server/queries-in/rdtype/name=AAAA
/isc/bind/statistics/server/queries-in/rdtype/counter=1112
```

Now, the output is finally very easy to manipulate with a standard utility like `sed` or `awk`.

4. Then, the next step to enquire from the locally installed agent is to add these two lines:

```
UserParameter=bind.queries.in[*],curl http://localhost:8053/ 2>/
dev/null | /usr/local/bin/xml2 | grep -A1 "/isc/bind/statistics/
server/queries-in/rdtype/name=$1$" | tail -1 | cut -d= -f2
UserParameter=bind.queries.out[*],curl http://localhost:8053/ 2>/
dev/null | /usr/local/bin/xml2 | grep -A1 "/isc/bind/statistics/
views/view/rdtype/name=$1$" | tail -1 | cut -d= -f2
```

Using the preceding command as an example, you can run the standard queries, such as A, AAAA, CNAME, ANY, MX, NS, PTR, SOA, and TXT records in/out.

Now, on the Zabbix server side, you need to configure all your items just as the one shown in the screenshot following the upcoming list, taking care to create the same kind of item for A as well:

- AAAA
- CNAME
- ANY

- MX

- NS

- PTR

- SOA

- TXT

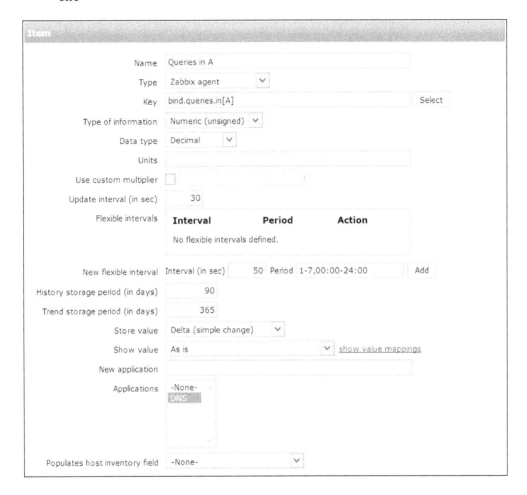

Once you've added all your items in a graph, the final result will be just like the one shown in the next screenshot. Now, you're acquiring all the queries done for the most important DNS fields.

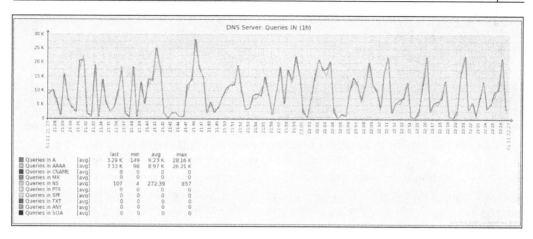

# DNS – response time

Now, we are monitoring all queries done against all the main DNS records, but actually we need to check how our DNS is working and then how much time is required to have the response back.

On the Zabbix how-to, there is an example to do what's available here: `https://www.zabbix.com/wiki/doku.php?id=howto/monitor/services/ monitor_dns_and_ntp_services_on_your_network`.

The problem with this example is that the script and code proposed simply *returns* a `0` or `1` depending on the DNS response or DNS timeout.

Well, that example is not good enough for us; we are looking for numbers like response time, and over those numbers we can implement a trigger. The trigger needs to go on fire when the time needed by DNS to give us back a response is higher than a value that we can consider acceptable. In a complex network, you can have a DNS query where you can *tolerate* a slow response (the entire development network segment, for instance, is not as critical as the production segment). Then, the solutions we propose here give us the response time. We can build our trigger over the response time unlike the other way, which is a lot less flexible.

We can see the script step by step; first of all, we need to acquire the response time. This can be done using dig, as follows:

```
#dig mydomain.com
```

> **NOTE**
>
> dig is part of the bind-utils package. If you don't have it installed in your system, you need to run as root the following command:
>
> **yum install bind-utils**

Anyway, dig uses the local resolver, and then if you run the same query again, you'll see that the time spent to acquire the DNS record is 0 minutes. This is clearly a false value! To avoid any cached response and to measure the real time, we need to use the +trace option. When tracing is enabled, dig makes iterative queries to resolve the name; practically, dig will follow referrals from the root servers, showing the answer from each server that was used to resolve the lookup.

Here, we need to have the total time spent for the query and not the time consumed by every server. To do that, we can use the following syntax:

```
$(time dig @127.0.0.1 mydomain.com +trace)
real     0m1.376s
user     0m0.010s
sys      0m0.012s
```

Now that we have understood the logic, here is the full script we will use:

```
# cat test_dns.sh
#!/bin/sh
if test -z "$1" ; then
    echo "You need to supply a DNS entry to check. Quitting"
    exit 01;
fi
DOMAIN=$1
MYTIME=$((time dig $DOMAIN +trace) 2>&1| grep real | awk -F'[m,s]'
'{print $2}')
if [ $? -eq 0 ]; then
  echo $MYTIME
else
  echo 0
fi
```

This script requires a $1 parameter, which is the domain to check. Now, we need to enable this script on the agent's side with UserParameter on the agent configuration file, thus adding:

```
UserParameter=dns.responsetime[*],test_dns.sh $1
```

The script we just created needs to placed in a valid runtime agent's path, or we need to use the fully qualified path in `UserParameter`, as follows:

```
UserParameter=dns.responsetime[*],/full/path/of/test_dns.sh $1
```

 This method is really useful as you can deploy the script on different network segments, like for instance, the application server zone, and have a real value of the time needed to resolve a DNS host from that network segment.

As the last step, create the relative item on the Zabbix server side, where you will pass the DNS name to check, as shown in the following screenshot:

Please bear in mind that this script, if executed continuously, can hammer your DNS exactly because it avoids using the cache of the local resolver and even one of the intermediate segments.

Then, as we have explained, we need to schedule our script with a reasonable period that can be for an instance of 1 minute. Please consider your network segments from which you're running this check, for both the quantity of scripts that are running and frequency.

 Here, you can create a trigger based on the zone, bearing in mind that you're monitoring the DNS response time directly from the hosts that require those DNS entries resolved. Here, it is important to tune your trigger based on the response time you consider acceptable from the point of view of the zone.

When you're creating your trigger, it is important to consider that this plugin provides you with the real DNS response time, which is the worst-case scenario. Here, we avoid using any caching systems, which is not the real case but a pessimistic one. That said, if you notice some spikes of high response time, those can be ignored as those spikes can't impact your system. Considering that, the trigger needs to be tuned to spot the response time that is still there for two or three item cycles (or even more – this depends on the frequency at which you run the check) and avoid considering single spikes.

# DNSSEC – monitoring the zone rollover

Here, we don't have enough pages to explain all the features added by DNSSEC or a complete setup guide of it. Anyway, it is important to know that the best way to avoid issues like a DNS cache poisoning attack is to use DNSSEC. DNSSEC does a deep usage of cryptographic keys and digital signatures to ensure that lookup data is correct and connections are legitimate. Then, in a secure environment, you're supposed to use mainly DNSSEC, and then it is important to monitor the critical DNSSEC parameters; those items can be resumed, as follows:

- The zonefile's validity
- The zones' rollover status
- The DNS response time

Currently, there are two plugins available to implement checks against the DNSSEC zone rollover:

- Rollstate
- Zonestate

The first one checks the zone managed by the daemon `rollerd`; the second one checks the validity of DNS zones.

 The full code is available at `https://github.com/hardaker/dnssec-tools/tree/master/dnssec-tools/apps/zabbix`, and the package is available at `http://www.dnssec-tools.org/download/dnssec-tools-2.1.tar.gz`.

One of the requirements to properly set up this plugin is that you need to be aware of the frequency of your rollover actions to tune the Zabbix item; please be aware that a little latency is normal here. Anyway, as long as you don't rollover zones every few minutes (TTL is set to a few minutes), this lag will not be an issue.

Now, before you can run the plugin, you need to have installed a few required **Perl** modules:

```
# perl -MCPAN -e shell
cpan>  install Net::DNS
cpan>  install Net::DNS::SEC
```

We are supposing that you already have `cpan` installed; if you don't have it installed in your system, please install it with the following line of code:

```
# yum install cpan
```

Now, once you have installed the required module, you need to install the `openssl-devel` package with the following command:

```
# yum install openssl-devel.x86_64
```

Now, you can finally uncompress the software with the following code:

```
# tar -zxvf ./dnssec-tools-2.1.tar.gz
# cd ./dnssec-tools-2.1
# ./configure && make && make install
```

Now in /dnssec-tools-2.1/apps/zabbix/, we have all the needed software. Here are the pieces of software available in /dnssec-tools-2.1/apps/zabbix/:

```
# ls -l
total 40
-rwxrwxr-x. 1 1274 1274  768 Jan  2 2013 backup-zabbix
-rw-rw-r--. 1 1274 1274 1706 Jan  2 2013 item.fields
-rw-rw-r--. 1 1274 1274 2878 Jan  2 2013 README
-rwxrwxr-x. 1 1274 1274 6763 Feb 15 2013 rollstate
-rwxrwxr-x. 1 1274 1274 7720 Feb 15 2013 uemstats
-rw-rw-r--. 1 1274 1274 1329 Oct 19 2011 zabbix_agentd.conf
-rwxrwxr-x. 1 1274 1274 6314 Feb 15 2013 zonestate
```

Finally, we can try our new plugins, as follows:

```
# ./rollstate mydomain.com
ZSK phase 3
# ./zonestate mydomain.com
zone file valid
```

Now, it's time to enable our new plugins; to do this, we need to define a couple of new entries of `UserParameter` on the agent side's /etc/zabbix/zabbix_agentd.conf:

```
UserParameter=dnssec-tools.rollover.status[*],rollstate $1
UserParameter=dnssec-tools.rollover.statusnum[*],rollstate –numeric $1
```

Even here, you need to place the `rollstate` plugin in a directory contained in the path or use the fully qualified path for our plugin. Also, once you have added `UserParameter`, you need to restart the agent with:

```
# service zabbix-agent restart
Shutting down Zabbix agent:                          [  OK  ]
Starting Zabbix agent:                               [  OK  ]
```

The `rollstate` plugin provides two different outputs with the `-numeric` option specified. It provides positive numbers for the ZSK phases and negative numbers for the KSK phases. This enables us to produce a graph that represents all the phases of DNSSEC.

Once you have created the Zabbix agent item on your template and your script is running, the output will be like the next screenshot.

In the example and the relative graph, we have a highly frequent rollover. In a real-life scenario, the time required to go through all the different statuses will be longer.

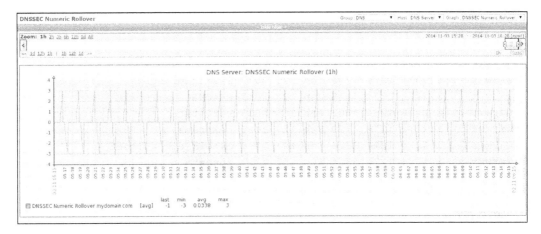

The details of the DNSSEC rollover in text mode, useful to keep track of all the status changes, will be contained in a text item. An example of the latest data is shown in the next screenshot:

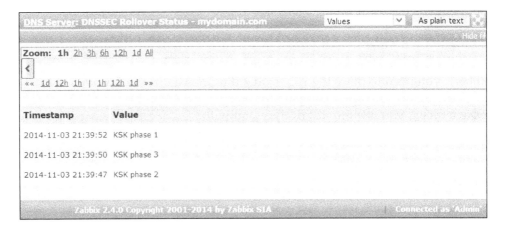

As you can see, you will have a historical status of all the steps crossed during the rollover, and you will have a clear track of the steps performed.

 This item will be precious if your process gets stuck on a step, especially if this happens periodically.

In the next screenshot, you can see the `zonestatus` plugin at work:

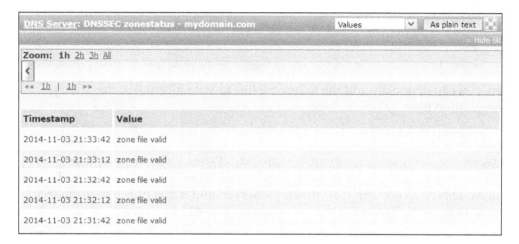

Now, the only thing you still have to do is create a trigger based on the information we're acquiring. Here, it is important to bear in mind that a little lag is normal during the zone transfer process; this lag needs to be considered when you set up the trigger.

# Apache monitoring

Most of the reverse proxies are nowadays implemented using Apache. Apache, other than being a web server, is quite useful as a reverse proxy as it includes some powerful modules:

- `mod_proxy`
- `mod_proxy_http`
- `mod_proxy_ftp`

Other than as a reverse proxy, it can be used as a load balancer thanks to:

- `mod_proxy_balancer`

Now, unfortunately, there isn't a valid method to acquire the metrics strictly related to the module used, but anyway, we can acquire quite a few metrics from Apache itself.

The first thing you have to do before you can acquire the statistics is enable them. To do this, you need to put the following lines in your Apache configuration file:

```
<Location /server-status>
  SetHandler server-status
  Allow from 127.0.0.1
  Order deny,allow
  Deny from all
</Location>
```

Also, you can optionally add the following line to your global Apache configuration file:

```
ExtendedStatus On
```

Here, we are configuring the module with the `ExtendedStatus On` option. With this setting, Apache keeps track of extended status information for each request. This collection can slow down the server, and if you notice performance issues, it can be disabled with the `ExtendedStatus Off` keyword.

> Please keep restricted, as much as you can, the access to the `/server-status` location. In our case, it is allowed only from `127.0.0.1`. This means that you need to collect the statistics from the agent installed locally on your Apache host. It is important to know that if `mod_status` is compiled into the server, then its handler is available in all configuration files, including per-directory files, like `htaccess`. This can have security-related ramifications for your site.

Now, all you have to do is restart your Apache and check whether you can retrieve the statistics running the following command:

```
[root@localhost ~]# curl http://127.0.0.1/server-status
<!DOCTYPE HTML PUBLIC "-//W3C//DTD HTML 3.2 Final//EN">
<html><head>
<title>Apache Status</title>
</head><body>
<h1>Apache Server Status for 127.0.0.1</h1>


<dl><dt>Server Version: Apache/2.2.15 (Unix) DAV/2 PHP/5.3.3</dt>
```

```
<dt>Server Built: Jul 23 2014 14:17:29
</dt></dl><hr /><dl>
<dt>Current Time: Monday, 03-Nov-2014 19:48:11 PST</dt>
<dt>Restart Time: Monday, 03-Nov-2014 19:48:00 PST</dt>
<dt>Parent Server Generation: 0</dt>
<dt>Server uptime:   11 seconds</dt>
<dt>Total accesses: 9 - Total Traffic: 0 kB</dt>
```

This Apache module's output is really full of useful information; looking at the output in detail, you can see that it provides the information shown in the following screenshot:

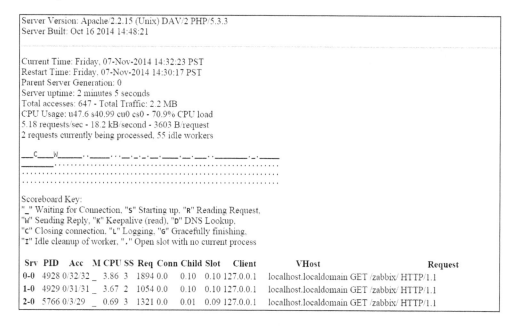

Here, you have a view that is split into four main sections, which are as follows:

- The Apache version data, module started, and server build details
- The Apache server status that provides you the uptime, CPU, number of access, number of request/sec, and some more information about its status
- The Apache scoreboard
- A section with all the details of the connection served

Here, retrieving the statistics is not as easy as you would imagine. The first and second sections are quite verbose, and it is easy to extract the required information from them once you've obtained the web page. The third section is a little more complex as it is the Apache scoreboard. The scoreboard is a representation of Apache's workers and their relative status. The workers are Apache's request-handler status. The keys used on the scoreboard are the following:

```
Scoreboard Key:
"_" Waiting for Connection, "S" Starting up, "R" Reading Request,
"W" Sending Reply, "K" Keepalive (read), "D" DNS Lookup,
"C" Closing connection, "L" Logging, "G" Gracefully finishing,
"I" Idle cleanup of worker, "." Open slot with no current process
```

Then, to retrieve and analyze the status, we need to use a slightly different URL: `http://localhost/server-status?auto`.

We can try the output produced by this URL using `curl`, as follows:

```
# curl  http://127.0.0.1/server-status?auto
Total Accesses: 1334
Total kBytes: 2163
CPULoad: 5.20713
Uptime: 2776
ReqPerSec: .480548
BytesPerSec: 797.879
BytesPerReq: 1660.35
BusyWorkers: 1
IdleWorkers: 10
Scoreboard: _____W___.............................................
............................................................
............................................................
...........................................
```

Now, it's easy to retrieve the `CPULoad` value, for instance:

```
# curl  -s http://127.0.0.1/server-status?auto |  awk '/^CPULoad:/ {print
$2}'
5.15882
```

With the same method, we can acquire all the metrics, for example, the number of `IdleWorkers` will be:

```
# curl  -s http://127.0.0.1/server-status?auto |  awk '/^IdleWorkers:/
{print $2}'
10
```

Parsing the scoreboard is a little different as we need to count the number of _ if we are looking at all the workers that are waiting for a connection instead of counting all the occurrences of W to check all the workers that are sending replies. To address this requirement, you can use the following command:

```
# curl  -s http://127.0.0.1/server-status?auto |  awk '/^Scoreboard:/
{print $2}'  | awk 'BEGIN { FS = "_" }; { print NF-1 }'
10
```

The first `awk` command identifies the `Scoreboard:` section, the second `awk` command counts all the occurrences of _ in the line, defining a field separator, and then counting all the matched fields.

Currently, there are three prebuilt plugins to do this:

- `zapache`: This is a shell script called via `UserParameter`
- `ZabbixApacheUpdater`: This is a Python software that needs to be scheduled on crontab
- `query_apachestats.py`: This is a Python software triggered by `UserParameter`

In this section, we will analyze `zapache` as it uses the same method described to acquire metrics from `mod_status` of Apache. The script is available for download at `https://github.com/lorf/zapache`.

All you have to do is download `zapache` from that location, copy `zapache` under `/home/zabbix/bin/` with the relative template, and then configure `UserParameter` in the agent configuration file `/etc/zabbix/zabbix_agentd.conf`, as shown here:

```
UserParameter=zapache[*],/home/zabbix/bin/zapache $1
```

Now, on the GUI, you have to create your template or import the one distributed with `zapache`. Then, navigate to **Configuration | Template | Import** and select the `zapache-template.xml` template if you want the item as *Zabbix agent* or the `zapache-template-active.xml` template if you prefer the items managed as *Zabbix agent (active)*.

If you take a look at the `zapache` source code, you will notice that it can run as Zabbix agent's mode or as an external script, which means that you can use it to acquire the Apache statistics locally on the same server or remotely.

Here is the code section that manages this kind of behavior:

```
if [[ $# ==  1 ]];then
  #Agent Mode
  STATUS_URL="http://127.0.0.1/server-status?auto"
```

```
      CASE_VALUE="$1"
 elif [[ $# == 2 ]];then
    #External Script Mode
    STATUS_URL="$1"
    case "$STATUS_URL" in
      http://*|https://*) ;;
      *) STATUS_URL="http://$STATUS_URL/server-status?auto";;
    esac
    CASE_VALUE="$2"
```

As you can see, you can run the script with only one parameter, which represents the metric you would like to acquire, or two parameters, specifying even the remote IP address of your Apache reverse proxy or web server. Here, in order to keep things easy, we avoid `mod_status` from being accessed externally using a `UserParameter`. Anyway, it is better to be aware that you can even centralize statistic acquisition thanks to this code section.

The final result of our setup and Apache's metric acquisition is shown in the next screenshot:

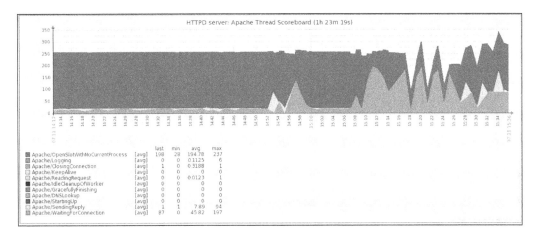

Now, it is time to discuss triggers related to this Apache monitoring. First of all, you need to create a trigger based on the last value of `zapache` ping, as follows:

```
{Template App Apache Web Server zapache:zapache[ping].last(0)}=0
```

Of course, if the `zapache` ping fails, returning `0`, you have an issue. Some other parameters that are critical for server status and on which you can create triggers are:

- `WaitingForConnection`: This indicates that the number of processes are waiting for a connection

- `ReqPerSec`: This indicates the number of requests per second
- `CPULoad`: This indicates the amount of CPU consumed by Apache

Those values are strictly dependent on the server you're using, the number of clients you are serving, and most importantly, what exactly and how you are serving the request. About what and how you are serving the request, you can have some very complex rewriting and reverse rules that can make a group of URLs more complex to manage. Here, the best thing to do is try to find out your Apache's limit using some tools that are able to produce a lot of concurrent connections and then workload, for instance, you can try Siege.

> More information about Siege is available here:
> `http://www.joedog.org/siege-home/`.

Once you've tested and found the maximum number of clients you can serve per URL and you've seen the web server limits, you can create and tune your custom triggers.

# NTP monitoring

The system clock is something you should keep monitoring because if, for some reason, your system suffers a system clock drift, this can become a big issue.

Performing a practical example of heavy drift on the system clock will cause issues. The DNSSEC zone replication, your FTP service, the IMAP service, and many other services will be affected, making your server unstable and unusable.

To keep your system clock in sync with the remote NTP, you can use and install the NTP daemon that will take care of the system clock.

To install NTP, you can use yum as usual:

```
# yum install ntp
... output removed here ...
Installed:
  ntp.x86_64 0:4.2.6p5-1.el6
Complete!
```

Once you've installed the NTP, you need to find the server that is closer to you using the website `http://www.pool.ntp.org/en/`.

From this website, you need to choose the server that is better for you and then change the `/etc/ntp.conf` configuration file.

Also, it is a good practice to add the log file directive at the end of the `ntp.conf` configuration file, as follows:

```
# echo "logfile /var/log/ntp.log" >> /etc/ntp.conf
```

Then start or restart the service, as follows:

```
# service ntpd stop
Shutting down ntpd:                        [  OK  ]
# service ntpd start
Starting ntpd:                             [  OK  ]
```

Now, you need to consider that you can have one central server used as a primary `ntpd` server for your network and propagate the system time from there; in this case, you need to change the `/etc/ntp.conf` configuration file a bit:

```
# Hosts on local network are less restricted.
restrict 192.168.1.0 mask 255.255.255.0 nomodify notrap
```

Now finally, you can attach all the hosts of your network to this `ntpd` server and then monitor this NTP and the client's time.

> If you are protecting a server with a firewall, you need to enable the UDP on port 123 on both directions. If you're using `iptables` to enable the client and the server communication, you need to add the following rules to the `OUTPUT` and `INPUT` chains:
>
> ```
> iptables -A INPUT -p udp --dport 123 -j ACCEPT
> iptables -A OUTPUT -p udp --sport 123 -j ACCEPT
> ```

Now, to retrieve metrics, we need to query `ntpd`. For this operation, we can use `ntpq`, which will show all the statistics. From a monitoring perspective, we're looking for the offset, jitter, and delay.

In the next example, we see the complete output of `ntpq`, as follows:

```
# ntpq -pn 127.0.0.1
Remote        refid        st t when poll reach   delay offset  jitter
================================================================
+91.247.253.152  191.241.139.137  3 u 9 64 1 35.276 29.492   9.791
+217.147.208.1   194.242.34.149   2 u 8 64 1 19.617 30.912  11.497
*192.33.214.47   129.194.21.195   2 u 7 64 1 25.581 32.157  11.007
+195.141.190.190 212.161.179.138  2 u 6 64 1 20.739 31.143  10.983
```

Please note that this server is suffering a big drift and the trigger is already on fire.

To acquire the metric then, we can use a command like this one:

```
# ntpq -pn 127.0.0.1 | /usr/bin/awk 'BEGIN { offset=0 } $1 ~/\*/ {
offset=$9 } END { print offset }'
32.157
```

This command retrieves the offset between the system clock and the NTP server.

> We are using the –p and –n options together; with the –n option,
> we are avoiding the name resolution, and then the DNS query.
> This is done in order to keep the item as lightweight as we can.

Now, we can quickly set up NTP monitoring using `UserParameter` on the agent side with:

```
UserParameter= ntp.jitter, ntpq -pn 127.0.0.1 | /usr/bin/awk 'BEGIN {
offset=0 } $1 ~/\*/ { offset=$9 } END { print offset }'
```

This will set `UserParameter` to retrieve the jitter value; anyway, we can even do something a little more complex and then produce a script like the following:

```
#!/bin/bash
VERSION="1.0"
function usage()
{
        echo "ntpcheck version: $VERSION"
        echo "usage:"
        echo "  $0 jitter          - Check ntp jitter delay"
        echo "  $0 offset          - Check ntp offset"
        echo "  $0 delay           - Check ntp delay"
}
########
# Main #
########
if [[ $# != 1 ]];then
        #No Parameter
        usage
        exit 0
fi
case "$1" in
'jitter')
        value="'ntpq -pn 127.0.0.1 | /usr/bin/awk 'BEGIN { jitter=0 }
$1 ~/\*/ { jitter=$10 } END { print jitter }'''"
        rval=$?;;
'offset')
```

```
        value="'ntpq -pn 127.0.0.1 | /usr/bin/awk 'BEGIN { offset=0 }
$1 ~/\*/ { offset=$9 } END { print offset }''"
        rval=$?;;
'delay')
        value="'ntpq -pn 127.0.0.1 | /usr/bin/awk 'BEGIN { delay=0 }
$1 ~/\*/ { delay=$8 } END { print delay }''"
        rval=$?;;
*)
        usage
        exit 1;;
esac

if [ "$rval" -eq 0 -a -z "$value" ]; then
        rval=1
fi

if [ "$rval" -ne 0 ]; then
        echo "ZBX_NOTSUPPORTED"
fi

echo $value
```

Then, on the agent side, we can deploy this script called `ntpcheck.sh` in the `/home/zabbix/bin` directory:

```
# ls -la /home/zabbix/bin/ntpcheck.sh
-rwxr-xr-x 1 zabbix zabbix 781 Nov 9 03:23 /home/zabbix/bin/ntpcheck.sh
```

Once this is done, all we have to do is create `UserParameter`, as follows:

```
UserParameter=ntp[*],/home/zabbix/bin/ntpcheck.sh $1
```

Then, restart the agent:

```
# service zabbix-agent restart
Shutting down Zabbix agent:                              [  OK  ]
Starting Zabbix agent:                                   [  OK  ]
```

Test our new items:

```
# zabbix_get -s 127.0.0.1 -k ntp[jitter]
2.273
# zabbix_get -s 127.0.0.1 -k ntp[offset]
-6.696
# zabbix_get -s 127.0.0.1 -k ntp[delay]
18.956
```

And in the end, create our three new items on the Zabbix GUI, as shown in the following screenshot:

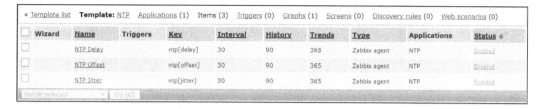

# NTP – what are we monitoring?

Now, even if those item names appear as something easy to understand, it is better to know what we are monitoring. First of all, we need to clarify that we're acquiring values for the current time source, hence we are taking the values in the line that begins with a * from the ntpq output. For convenience, the ntpq output is reported here:

```
# ntpq -pn 127.0.0.1
Remote       refid       st t when poll reach   delay offset  jitter
==================================================================
+91.247.253.152   191.241.139.137   3 u 9 64 1 35.276 29.492   9.791
+217.147.208.1    194.242.34.149    2 u 8 64 1 19.617 30.912  11.497
*192.33.214.47    129.194.21.195    2 u 7 64 1 25.581 32.157  11.007
+195.141.190.190 212.161.179.138    2 u 6 64 1 20.739 31.143  10.983
```

As you can see, the lines of this output are not ordered, and they begin with + and * (in this example). We are interested in the one that begins with *. The reason is that the line that begins with * represents the preferred and current time source.

We can even have a prefix like the following:

- +: This sign indicates that the peer is a good, preferred remote peer or server
- (space), x, -, #, and .: These indicate that this peer is not being used for synchronization

Now, we have clarified the reason why we are running this awk command:

```
# ntpq -pn 127.0.0.1 | /usr/bin/awk 'BEGIN { delay=0 } $1 ~/\*/ {
delay=$8 } END { print delay }'
```

Now, to have some more details about what we're acquiring, we can define them as:

- **Delay**: This is the current estimated delay. It is the transit time between remote peers or servers in milliseconds.

- **Offset**: This is the current estimated offset. It is the time difference between remote peers in milliseconds.

- **Jitter**: This is the current estimated dispersion, or better, the variation in delay between these peers in milliseconds.

 If you're monitoring a server that is running in a virtual environment, you need to be aware that practically all the virtualization software suffers from system clock drift. Then check the vendor-specific best practice to reduce the NTP drift.

Now it's time to change the script a little as we can check the NTP health status by adding the following case statement:

```
case "$1" in
...
'health')
        primary="'ntpq -pn 127.0.01 | grep ^\* |grep -v grep | wc -l'"
        rval=$?
        if [ "${primary}" -eq "1" ] ; then
                value="1"
        else
                value="0"
        fi
        ;;
...
esac
```

Now, we can check whether we have at least one primary preferred source defined to get the NTP sync in a good shape. We need to then add a new item and a related trigger that will go on fire if the value returned is 0. Other than this trigger, we can even have a trigger that will go on fire if the clock drift is bigger than 50 milliseconds for instance, or even less.

In the next screenshot, you see the interaction between the **Jitter**, **Offset**, and **Delay** on a Linux virtual server (that suffer from big system clock drifts):

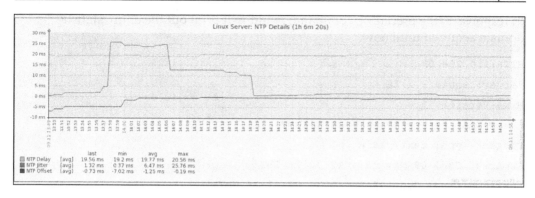

# Squid monitoring

Squid is the most diffused caching proxy for the Web. Squid supports HTTP, HTTPS, FTP, and many more protocols. This proxy software reduces a lot of the bandwidth required to serve its clients and improves the response time, implementing a very good caching system. For all those reasons, it is quite evident why you should have Squid to monitor inside your network.

There are two primary ways to acquire data and metrics from Squid:

- Using SNMP
- Using `squidclient`

If you're curious about the SNMP setup on the Squid server, you can have a look at the official documentation, in particular the section available at `http://wiki.squid-cache.org/Features/Snmp`.

We should avoid enabling SNMP on our Squid as it has been affected in the past by many overflows and issues. The last security issue, at the time of writing this, caused by SNMP enabled on Squid, is available at `http://www.squid-cache.org/Advisories/SQUID-2014_3.txt`, and as you can see, it is a really recent issue.

Fortunately, the client is really powerful and this permits us to implement a good monitoring solution without enabling SNMP.

Type the following command:

```
# squidclient mgr:info
```

In response to the preceding command, Squid will print out the entire statistic domain acquired until now:

```
HTTP/1.0 200 OK
Server: squid/3.1.10
Mime-Version: 1.0
Date: Sun, 09 Nov 2014 17:23:25 GMT
Content-Type: text/plain
Expires: Sun, 09 Nov 2014 17:23:25 GMT
Last-Modified: Sun, 09 Nov 2014 17:23:25 GMT
X-Cache: MISS from localhost.localdomain
X-Cache-Lookup: MISS from localhost.localdomain:3128
Via: 1.0 localhost.localdomain (squid/3.1.10)
Connection: close
...
```

Then, as you can understand, it will be quite easy to retrieve some important items from this kind of output. Trying out an example, if you would like to acquire the CPU Usage, you can simply run:

```
# squidclient mgr:info|grep 'CPU Usage:'
        CPU Usage:        0.01%
```

Of course, this kind of output needs to be a little shaped to be usable for our work, the next command will be a UserParameter ready command:

```
# squidclient mgr:info|grep 'CPU Usage:'|cut -d':' -f2|tr -d '%'|tr -d '
\t'
0.01
```

Now, we have two ways of doing this:

- We create a long list of UserParameter on the agent side
- We create just a one-user UserParameter and call it using a parameter

The second way is the preferred approach as if you need to add an item to acquire, you don't need to restart the agent. Here due to space constraints, we will not comment all the script; for the complete script, please refer to *Appendix B, Collecting Squid Metrics*.

You need to create UserParameter:

```
UserParameter=squid[*],/home/zabbix/bin/squidcheck.sh $1
```

Now, you need to restart the agent, and you can check whether you're able to acquire the metrics with the following command:

```
# zabbix_get -s 127.0.0.1 -k squid[icp_sent]
12
```

If you can retrieve the metrics, the configuration is fine.

Now, on the server side, you need to create your items, as shown in the following screenshot:

| Wizard | Name | Triggers | Key | Interval | History | Trends | Type | Applications | Status ↓ |
|---|---|---|---|---|---|---|---|---|---|
| | Squid: Process memory usage | | squid[process_mem] | 60 | 30 | 365 | Zabbix agent | Squid | Enabled |
| | Squid: Request disk hit ratio 5 mins | | squid[request_disk_hit_ratio_5] | 60 | 30 | 365 | Zabbix agent | Squid | Enabled |
| | Squid: Mean object size | | squid[mean_obj_size] | 60 | 30 | 365 | Zabbix agent | Squid | Enabled |
| | Squid: Number of ICP messages sent | | squid[icp_sent] | 60 | 30 | 365 | Zabbix agent | Squid | Enabled |
| | Squid: Number of ICP messages received | | squid[icp_received] | 60 | 30 | 365 | Zabbix agent | Squid | Enabled |
| | Squid: Request hit ratio | | squid[request_hit_ratio] | 60 | 30 | 365 | Zabbix agent | Squid | Enabled |
| | Squid: Request memory hit ratio 5 mins | | squid[request_mem_hit_ratio_5] | 60 | 30 | 365 | Zabbix agent | Squid | Enabled |
| | Squid: Request memory hit ratio 60 mins | | squid[request_mem_hit_ratio_60] | 60 | 30 | 365 | Zabbix agent | Squid | Enabled |
| | Squid: Byte hit ratio 60 mins | | squid[byte_hit_ratio_60] | 60 | 30 | 365 | Zabbix agent | Squid | Enabled |
| | Squid: Request disk hit ratio 60 mins | | squid[request_disk_hit_ratio_60] | 60 | 30 | 365 | Zabbix agent | Squid | Enabled |
| | Squid: Service time all HTTP requests | | squid[servicetime_httpreq] | 60 | 30 | 365 | Zabbix agent | Squid | Enabled |
| | Squid: Request failure ratio | | squid[req_fail_ratio] | 60 | 30 | 365 | Zabbix agent | Squid | Enabled |
| | Squid: Number of ICP messages queued | | squid[icp_queued] | 60 | 30 | 365 | Zabbix agent | Squid | Enabled |
| | Squid: Number of HTTP requests received/sec | | squid[http_requests] | 60 | 30 | 365 | Zabbix agent | Squid | Enabled |
| | Squid: Cache size on disk | | squid[cache_size_disk] | 60 | 30 | 365 | Zabbix agent | Squid | Enabled |
| | Squid: Cache size in memory | | squid[cache_size_mem] | 60 | 30 | 365 | Zabbix agent | Squid | Enabled |
| | Squid: Byte hit ratio 5 mins | | squid[byte_hit_ratio_5] | 60 | 30 | 365 | Zabbix agent | Squid | Enabled |
| | Squid: Average ICP messages per minute | | squid[avg_icp_msg_per_min] | 60 | 30 | 365 | Zabbix agent | Squid | Enabled |
| | Squid: Average HTTP requests per minute | | squid[avg_http_req_per_min] | 60 | 30 | 365 | Zabbix agent | Squid | Enabled |
| | Squid: Number of connected clients | | squid[clients] | 60 | 30 | 365 | Zabbix agent | Squid | Enabled |
| | Squid: CPU usage | | squid[cpu_usage] | 60 | 30 | 365 | Zabbix agent | Squid | Enabled |
| | Squid: Number of HTCP messages sent | | squid[htcp_sent] | 60 | 30 | 365 | Zabbix agent | Squid | Enabled |
| | Squid: Number of HTCP messages received | | squid[htcp_received] | 60 | 30 | 365 | Zabbix agent | Squid | Enabled |
| | Squid: File descriptors configured | | squid[filedescr_max] | 60 | 30 | 365 | Zabbix agent | Squid | Enabled |
| | Squid: File descriptors available | Triggers (1) | squid[filedescr_avail] | 60 | 30 | 365 | Zabbix agent | Squid | Enabled |
| | Squid: Processes running | Triggers (1) | proc.num[squid] | 60 | 30 | 365 | Zabbix agent | Squid | Enabled |

Now that we are finally acquiring all the metrics, it is important to define at least two triggers:

- One tied to the number of Squid processes running that should never be 0
- One tied to the number of available file descriptors; if this number is less than 100, we need to have a trigger on fire

This is shown in the following screenshot and is the minimum number of triggers you should have:

| | Severity | Name ↑ | Expression | | Status |
|---|---|---|---|---|---|
| | High | Squid: Process not running | {Template_Squid/done/proc.num[squid].last(0)}=0 | | Enabled |
| | Average | Squid: Running out of file descriptors | {Template_Squid/done/squid[filedescr_avail].last(0)}<100 | | Enabled |

To close the Squid monitoring, we can tell that you are now able to acquire at least 22 items using the script available on GitHub at `https://github.com/smartmarmot/zabbix_network_monitoring/tree/master/Chapter3`; you can now set many other triggers depending on your setup, server capacity, number of clients to serve, and the mean of the number of pages required by your client network.

Among the most important parameters to monitor, we have:

- The byte hit ratio over 5 and 60 minutes
- The request disk hit ratio over 5 and 60 minutes
- Request failure ratio

All the hit ratios need to be as close to 100 percent as possible. Every value of caching under 70 percent should make a trigger go on fire, and even the **request failure ratio**, if it is higher than 30, should trigger an alarm as it is telling us that our system is not responding properly.

# Summary

In this chapter, we covered a large number of components. We started our discussion from the most used and even very critical network service: DNS. Going ahead on the same way, we discussed DNSSEC; then, we moved on to Apache, the most used and effective reverse proxy; walked through NTP; and closed the chapter with Squid, the most installed and used proxy service. For all the systems and services analyzed, you're now able to acquire the most critical metrics, and you know how to create effective triggers.

Triggers here are covering the most critical role and hence your experience within your network is the truly added value. You, with the knowledge acquired from this chapter and your environment experience, will be the key to creating effective and proactive triggers. This chapter has covered all the critical services you can find in a network, and now you can easily provide a heavy added value, creating proactive checks and installing an effective, tailor-made monitoring solution. In the next chapter, you will learn how to automate the discovering of your network's elements and how to apply a template to the discovered item. Also, you have to adapt your monitoring system within your environments, and this kind of task is the typical boring and time-consuming task that a network admin doesn't like to do. The chapter will provide you with all the necessary information to use the host discovery and the low-level discovery in an effective way. You will be guided through the difficult way to automate the item discovery: this will heavily reduce the time needed to start up your monitoring solution but will impact and reduce the time needed to maintain your growing and dynamically moving setup.

# 4
# Discovering Your Network

In the previous chapters, we've seen how to get different metrics from quite a few different sources, using different methods. What we haven't covered yet, is how to easily get all this data into Zabbix when you have a great number of monitored objects.

Manually creating hosts, items, and triggers is an excellent exercise to get the hang of how things work in Zabbix, but it can quickly become a repetitive, boring, error-prone activity. In other words, they are the kinds of tasks computers were made for in the first place.

What if your monitoring solution could just find the hosts and devices you want to monitor, add them as Zabbix hosts, apply a template, and start monitoring them? And what if it didn't just limit itself to finding hosts to monitor, but it also found out whether your switch has 24 or 48 ports, how many disks your web server has attached, and what ports are open on a certain host? After some initial configuration, you would not have to bother with adding or removing things to monitor. It would certainly be great, but the problem with automated discovery is that it often has to come to terms with the reality of a real-world network, which is often full of exceptions and special rules. In such cases, you could find yourself spending a lot of time trying to adapt your monitoring system to your environment in order to catch up with an automated discovery that might be just a little too automatic.

Luckily, Zabbix can support many different discovery strategies, mix them up with regular host and item creation, and generally provide a good balance between the need to have a fully automated system and the need do have a monitoring solution that matches as closely as possible the environment it has to monitor, with all its exceptions and special cases that are impossible to capture with just a discovery strategy.

This chapter will be divided into two main parts that mirror the two main levels of discovery that Zabbix supports: **network discovery** and **low-level discovery**. The former is used to find out which hosts are in your network, and the latter is used to find out what facilities and components are featured in a given host.

Let's start with finding out how network discovery works and how to make the most out of it.

# Finding hosts the Zabbix way

Zabbix's discovery facilities consist of a set of rules that periodically scan the network, looking for new hosts, or disappearing ones, according to predetermined conditions.

The three methods Zabbix can use to check for new or disappeared hosts, given an IP range, are:

- The availability of a Zabbix agent
- The availability of an SNMP agent
- The response to simple external checks (FTP, SSH, and so on)

These checks can also be combined, as illustrated in the following example:

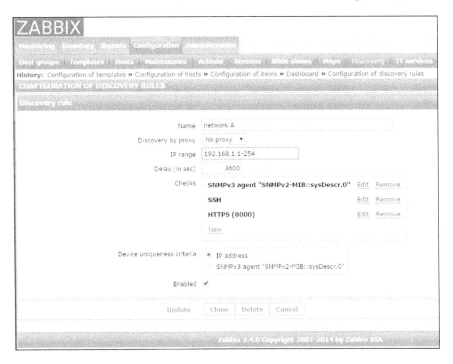

As you can see, when enabled, this rule will check every hour, in the IP range `192.168.1.1-254`, for any server that:

- Returns an SNMPv3 value for the `SNMPv2-MIB::sysDescr.0` OID
- Is listening to and accepting connections via SSH
- Has an HTTPS server listening on port `8000`

Be aware that a discovery event will be generated if any one of these conditions is met. So, if a discovery rule has three checks defined and a host in the network responds to all three checks, three events will be generated, one per service.

As usual with all things Zabbix, a discovery rule will not do anything by itself, except generate a discovery event. It will then be the job of Zabbix's actions facility to detect the aforesaid event and decide whether and how to act on it.

Discovery event actions are very similar to regular trigger event actions, so you'll probably be already able to make the most out of them. The main thing to remember is that with Zabbix, you cannot act directly on an event to create or disable a host: you need to either copy the event data by hand somewhere and then proceed with all the manual operations needed based on that data, or you need to properly configure some actions to do that work for you. In other words, without a properly configured action, a discovery rule will not add by itself any discovered host to the list of monitored ones.

Every action has a global scope: it's not tied to any particular trigger, host, or host group by default. This means that when you create an action, you'll need to provide some action conditions in order to make it valid only for certain events and not others. To access the discovery actions section in the web UI, head to **Configuration | Actions** and then select **Discovery** from the **Event** source drop-down menu, just under the **Create action** button.

When you create an action, you'll start with giving it a name and defining a default message in the **action definition** section. You'll then move to the **action conditions** section to provide filtering intelligence, before finishing with the **action operations** section to provide the action's core functionality. Action definitions are pretty simple as you'll just need to provide a unique name for the action and a default message, if you need one. So, let's move straight to the interesting sections of action configuration: conditions and operations.

# Defining action conditions

The **action conditions** section lets you define conditions based on the event's reported host IP address, service status and reported value, discovery rules, and a few others:

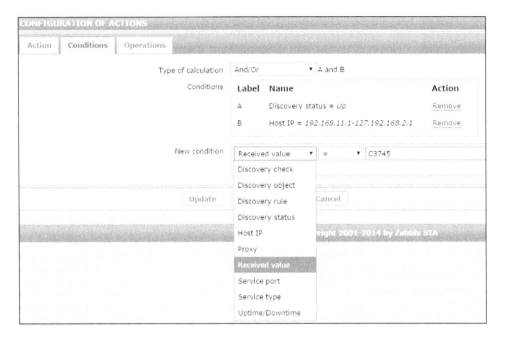

The **Received value** condition is of particular interest, as it allows you to do things like differentiating between operating systems, application versions, and any other information you could get from a Zabbix or SNMP agent query. This will be invaluable when defining action operations, as you'll see in the next paragraph. A received value depends on the discovery rule and on the output of the discovery event that triggers the action. For example, if a discovery rule is set to look for hosts responding to an SNMP Get for the SNMPv2-MIB::sysDescr.0 OID, and that rule finds a router that has C3745 as the value of that OID, then the discovery event will pass C3745 to the action as the received value.

Single conditions can be combined together with logical operators. There's not much flexibility in how you can combine them though.

You can either have all AND, all OR, or a combination of the two where conditions of different types are combined with AND, while conditions of the same type are combined with OR.

# Choosing action operations

Discovery actions are somewhat simpler than trigger actions as there are no steps or escalations involved. This doesn't mean that you don't have quite a few options to choose from:

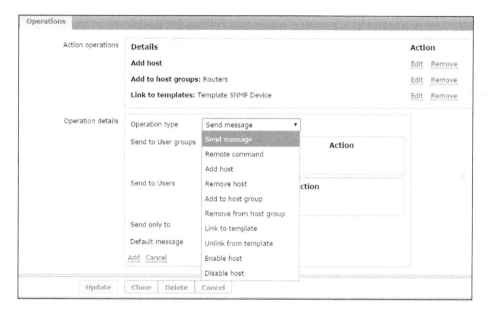

Please note that even if you defined a default message, it won't be sent until you specify the recipients in this section using the **Send message** operation. On the other hand, if adding (or removing) a host is a quite self-explanatory action, when it comes to adding to a host group or linking to a template, it becomes clear that a good set of actions with specific received value conditions and template-linking operations can give a high level of automation to your Zabbix installation.

This high level of automation is probably more useful in rapidly changing environments that still display a good level of predictability, for example, the kind of hosts you can find, such as fast-growing grids or clusters. In these kinds of environments, you can have new hosts appearing on a daily basis, and maybe old hosts disappear at almost the same rate, but the kind of host is more or less always the same. This is the ideal premise for a small set of well-configured discovery rules and actions, so you don't have to constantly and manually add or remove the same types of hosts. On the other hand, if your environment is quite stable or you have a very high host type variability, you might want to look more closely at which, and how many hosts, you are monitoring as any error can be much more critical in such environments.

Also, limiting discovery actions to sending messages about discovered hosts can prove quite useful in such chaotic environments or where you don't control directly your systems' inventory and deployment. In such cases, getting simple alerts about new hosts, or disappearing ones, can help the monitoring team keep Zabbix updated despite any communication failure between IT departments, accidental or otherwise.

Moreover, you are not stuck with e-mails and SMSes for notifications or logging. In an **Action** operation form, you can only choose recipients as Zabbix users and groups. If the users don't have any media defined, or they don't have the right media for the action operation, they won't receive any message. Adding media to users is done through the **Administration** tab of the Zabbix frontend, where you can also specify a time window for a specific media to be used (so that you won't get discovery messages as an SMS in the middle of the night for example). Speaking of users and media types, you can also define custom ones, through the **Media types** section of the **Administration** tab in Zabbix's frontend. New media types will be available both in the **Media section** of the user configuration and as targets for message sending in the **Action** operations form.

An interesting use for new media types is to define custom scripts that can go beyond simple email or SMS sending.

A custom media script has to reside on the Zabbix server, in the directory indicated by the `AlertScriptsPath` variable, in the `zabbix_server.conf` configuration file. When called upon, it will be executed with three parameters passed by the server and taken from the action configuration in the context of the event that was generated:

- `$1`: This is the recipient of the message
- `$2`: This is the subject of the message
- `$3`: This is the main message body

The recipient's address will be the one defined for the new media type in the corresponding media property for the user specified in the action operation step. The subject and the message body will also be passed according to the action operation step, as shown in the preceding list. This is all that Zabbix needs to know about the script.

The fact is, a custom script can actually do many different things with the message: logging to a local or remote directory, creating an XML document and interacting with a log manager web services API, printing on a custom display—just as with every custom solution, the sky's the limit with custom media types.

Here is a simple, practical example of such a custom media type. Let's say that your IT department has implemented a self-provisioning service for virtual machines so that developers and system admins can create their own VMs and use them for a limited amount of time before they are destroyed and the resources recycled. This laboratory of sorts has been put in a separate network, but users still have to gain access to it, and they are also administrators of those VMs, so there's very little control over what gets installed, configured, or uninstalled on those machines. In other words, while you could provision the VMs with a preinstalled Zabbix agent, you can't really rely on the fact that your users, whether inadvertently or for specific reasons, would not disable it, or would not install services that should really not be there, like a DHCP server for example. So, you decide to keep an eye on those machines directly from the Zabbix server (or a suitable proxy) and implement a simple discovery rule that will generate a discovery event for every host that responds to an ICMP echo request and nothing more, as follows:

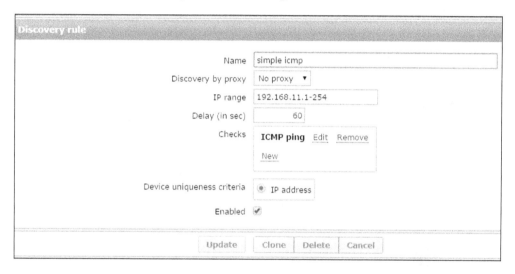

Based on that rule, you'll want to configure an action that, for every host in that subnet, will perform a port scan and report the results via mail to you.

To do that, you'll first need to have a custom media type and the corresponding script. So, you head to **Administration | Media types** and click on **Create media type**. Once there, you assign a suitable name, select **Script** as a type and provide Zabbix with the name of the script to execute. Here, you just need to define the script name, as shown in the following screenshot. You'll find out later in the chapter in what directory the actual script should be placed:

Just adding a media type is not enough though, you'll have to enable it for the user you intend to send those reports to. Just head to **Administration | Users** and select the user you want to add the new media type to. Quite predictably, the tab you want is called **Media**. Add the media you just created and remember to also add a way to tell the script where it should send the results. Since you are interested in receiving an e-mail address after all, that's what we'll tell Zabbix, as follows:

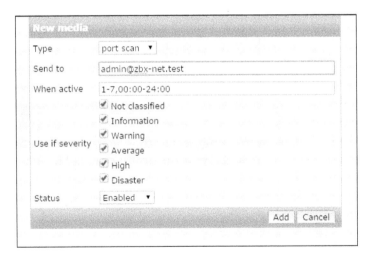

The **Send to** parameter will be the first argument passed to port_scan.sh, followed by the subject and the body of the message to send. So, before actually deploying the script, let's define the subject and the body of the message. To do that, you'll need to create an action for the discovery event, as follows:

For the purposes of the script, all you really need is the IP address of the host you are going to scan, but it certainly wouldn't hurt to add some more information in the final message.

The next step is to define some conditions for the action. Remember that actions are global, so the first condition you want to set is the IP range on which this action will be performed, otherwise you'd run the risk of performing a port scan on every discovered host in your network.

You might also want to limit the action as a consequence for the discovery rule you created, independent of any other rules you might have on the same network.

Finally, you should make a decision about the discovery status. If you want a periodic update of what ports are open on a discovered host, you'll also need to define a condition for the host to be **Up**: in other words, for the host to be reported as live for at least two consecutive checks.

For as long as the host stays up, a port scan will be executed and reported according to the discovery interval of the rule you defined earlier. If you just want a port scan for a new host or for a host that has been reported as down for a while, you'll just need to fire the action on the condition that the host is **Discovered**; that is, it is now being reported up, while it was down before. What is certain is that you'll want to avoid any action if the host is down or unavailable.

The following screenshot encapsulates the discussion in this paragraph:

The last step is to define the action operation that is sending the message via the port_scan custom media type to the user you want, as follows:

Once done with this, you are finally ready to create the `port_scan.sh` script. So, head to the `AlertScriptsPath` directory as configured in your `zabbix_server.conf` (it's usually defined as `/usr/lib/zabbix/alertscripts`) and create the following script there:

```
#!/bin/bash

RECIPIENT=$1
IPADDRESS=$2
MESSAGE=$3

SCAN="nmap -AT5 -sT"

RESULT=$($SCAN $IPADDRESS)

(echo "Scan results for IP $IPADDRESS";
echo "$RESULT";
echo "";
echo "$MESSAGE") | mailx -s "Scan results for $IPADDRESS" $RECIPIENT
```

> Don't forget to set the correct ownership and permissions for the script once you are done:
> ```
> # chown zabbix port_scan.sh
> # chmod 755 port_scan.sh
> ```

As you can see, the program that will perform the actual port scan is **Nmap,** so make sure you have it installed. In case you don't have it installed, a simple `yum install nmap` will take care of that. The options passed to Nmap are just the basics: `-sT` performs a simple `connect()` scan. It's not the fanciest one, but it's the only one available to non-root users, and the script will be executed by Zabbix as the `zabbix` user. `-A` turns on traceroute, OS, and service detection so that the output is as complete as possible. Finally, `-T5` forces Nmap to execute the port scan in as little time as possible. Once the script has the results of the port scan, it will just construct the message and send it to the recipient defined in the action.

This is, of course, a very basic script, but it will get the job done, and you'll soon receive a port scan report for every new VM created in your self-provisioning lab. To keep things simple and clear, we did not include any consistency checking or error reporting in case of problems, so that's certainly a way you can improve on this example. You could also try to send the results to a log file (or a log directory) instead of a mail address, or even to a database, so that other automation components can pick up the reports and make them available via other media such as web pages. What you'll probably want to avoid is to directly change the host's configuration, or Zabbix's own one, through this script.

Even if no one will prevent you from doing so, it's probably best if you avoid using all this power to execute complex scripts that might change your network configuration, such as enabling interfaces, adding rules to a firewall, and such like. While this is perfectly possible using a custom media script, this should be the domain of remote commands. These will take center stage in the next paragraph.

# Remote commands

There are quite a few options available to you when it comes to executing remote commands as an action operation.

You can define a list of IPMI commands to be run on the target host or a series of SSH commands that connect to a box and perform various operations there. A remote command could even be a simple wrapper for a remote script deployed on a Zabbix agent, or a custom script that will be run either on an agent or on the Zabbix server itself.

The truth is, sometimes, remote commands can be just a little too powerful. You can start and stop services, deploy or provision software, make configuration changes, open or close firewall ports, and everything else you can possibly imagine, as long as you can write a script for it. While this can sound fascinating and promising, we have found over the years that these solutions tend to be fragile and unpredictable. One of the reasons is that Zabbix doesn't warn you if a remote command fails. More importantly, environments tend to change faster than these automation tools so that you can quickly find yourself dealing with the unintended consequences of a remote command running where it should not run, or not running when it should run.

The more of these you add, the more it will be hard to keep track of them, and the more one can be lured into a false sense of security, counting on the fact that remote commands are taking care of things, while, in fact, they may be contributing to the chaos instead of taming it.

That said, it's certainly undeniable that remote commands can be useful. Let's see an example that is both helpful for your Zabbix configuration and also fairly safe.

In *Chapter 2, Active Monitoring of Your Devices*, we've seen how it's possible to use some of the measurements, as reported by a host's items, to populate the same host's inventory fields. This is a great solution for the fields that can be filled this way, but what about the other ones? Things like POC details, maintenance dates, installer name, installed software, and such like can't always be extrapolated from monitoring metrics as they may simply not be available on the monitored host itself.

They usually are available, though, on asset inventory systems that IT departments use to keep track of available resources.

In the following example, you'll create an action operation that will execute a remote command on the Zabbix server, fetch some inventory information from an asset database, and fill up or update the host's inventory details.

Before proceeding with the command, let's make an assumption and some preparations.

There are many asset inventory systems available, some proprietary and some open source. All of them have different database schemas and different ways to expose their data. Moreover, an inventory database structure depends as much on the actual environment it's put into, and the processes that govern the aforesaid environment, as it is on its internal specifications. So, we decided to use a dummy asset management tool that will return, given an IP address, a simple JSON object containing all the inventory data you need for the task at hand. The assumption is that you'll be able to put the example into your context and figure out how to extract the same information from your own inventory management system, and that you will also know what authentication scheme you will rely on if you need to make just one request or multiple related requests, and so on.

Secondly, for practical reasons we are going to use Python as the language of the command script, so you'll want to make sure that it's installed and available on your Zabbix server. If it's not there, you can install it, and the related utilities, quite easily using `yum`:

```
# yum install python
# yum install python-setuptools
# easy_install pip
```

Finally, we are going to interact with Zabbix's configuration not through direct queries to its database, but through its API. In order to do that, we'll use a very useful Python library, called **pyzabbix**. You can find it at `https://github.com/lukecyca/pyzabbix`, but since you installed `pip`, it will be extremely easy to make it available to your Python installation. Just run the following command:

```
# pip install pyzabbix
```

The Python package manager will download and install it for you.

Now we are ready to configure the discovery action and write the actual command script.

You can choose to reuse an existing discovery rule, such as the simple ICMP rule you used in the previous paragraph, you can create a new one specific to a single network to scan, a single TCP port that has to be available, or the presence of a Zabbix agent. We won't go into any more details here, as you've already learned how to configure one earlier in the chapter. Similarly, we can safely skip any detail about the action conditions as they might also be entirely similar to those shown earlier. What changes is, of course, the action operation. The following screenshot will give you a better idea of what we have been talking about in this paragraph:

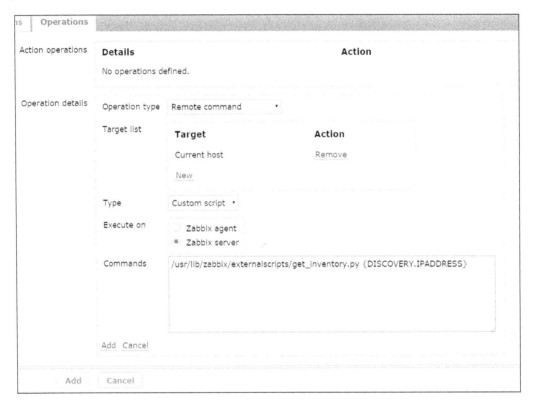

The important elements here are the fact that the script should be executed on the Zabbix server, the fact that we specified the full path for the script, and the fact that we are using the {DISCOVERY.IPADDRESS} macro as the argument.

Once the action is configured, you are ready to prepare the actual script. Let's see how it would look:

```python
#!/usr/bin/python
import sys
import json
from pyzabbix import ZabbixAPI
```

```
import dummy_inventory_api

ipaddr = sys.argv[1]

hostinfo_json = dummy_inventory_api.getinfo(ipaddr)
# hostinfo_json will contain a JSON string similar to this one:
# { "hostip"      : "172.16.11.11",
#    "hostname"   : "HostA",
#    "inventory"  : {
#            "asset_tag"       : "12345678",
#            "install_date"    : "31-11-2014",
#            "installer_name": "SKL"
#            }
# }

hostinv = json.loads(hostinfo_json)['inventory']

zbx = ZabbixAPI(http://127.0.0.1/zabbix/)
zbx.login("admin", "zabbix")
hostinfo = zbx.host.get(output=['hostid'], filter={'ip': ipaddr})
hid = hostinfo[0]['hostid]
zbx_inventory = {
                    'date_hw_install': hostinv['install_date'],
                    'installer_name' : hostinv['installer_name'],
                    'asset_tag'       : '12345678'
                  # add other fields you may be interested in…
                }
zbx.host.update(hostid=hid, inventory=zbx_inventory)
sys.exit()
```

As you can see, the script is fairly straightforward and simplistic, but it can be used as a starting point for your own inventory-updating scripts. The main thing that you need to take care of is to figure out how to get your inventory data from your asset database. You might need to connect to a REST API, or get an XML document via a web service, or even perform some queries via ODBC. What matters is that you end up with a Python dictionary or list containing all that you need to update the relevant host in Zabbix.

The second part of the script first of all shows you how to connect to the Zabbix API using the ZabbixAPI constructor. It then proceeds with the login method, where you'll need to provide the credentials you configured earlier.

All `get` methods accept a `filter` parameter that you can use to retrieve a single object or a list of objects that satisfy certain conditions. In this case, we used it to get the `hostid` of the host that is associated with a specific IP address.

Pay attention to the next line as the value returned by all `get` methods is always a list, even if it contains only one element. That's why we need to reference the first element of `hostinfo`, element `0`, before referencing the `inventory` dictionary key.

We only showed three inventory fields here, but there are many more available in Zabbix, so it may be a good idea to build a dictionary with all Zabbix inventory fields as keys and the retrieved values as values.

Now that we have the `hostid` and the inventory information at our disposal, we can proceed with the actual inventory update. The update method is fairly straightforward: you specify the `hostid` of the host you want to update and the new values for the fields that you need to update.

And that's it, with a script like this configured as a remote command for a discovery action, you can keep your Zabbix inventory data in sync with whatever asset management system you may have.

As you might have realized, host discovery can be quite a complex matter because of the sheer number of variables you need to take care of, and because it's not always easy, in a real-world network, to identify a clear logic for host creation, template assignment, and other monitoring parameters, based on discovery data.

Low-level discovery, by contrast, is much more simple, given its power to dynamically create specific items as a host's available resources are discovered. So, let's use the remaining pages of this chapter to explore a few aspects of this extremely useful feature.

# Low-level discovery

An extremely useful and important feature of Zabbix templates is their ability to support special kinds of items called low-level discovery rules. Once applied to actual hosts, these rules will query the host for whatever kind of resources they are configured to look for: filesystems, network interfaces, SNMP OIDs, and more. For every resource found, the server will dynamically create items, triggers, and graphs according to special entity prototypes connected to the discovery rules.

The great advantage of low-level discovery rules is that they take care of the more variable parts of a monitored host, such as the type and number of network interfaces, in a dynamic and general way. This means that, instead of manually creating specific items and triggers of every host's network interfaces or filesystems, or creating huge templates with any possible kind of item for a particular operating system and keeping most of these items disabled, you can have a reasonable number of general templates that will adapt themselves to the specifics of any given host by creating on the fly any entity required, based on discovered resources and previously configured prototypes.

Out of the box, Zabbix supports four discovery rules:

- Network interfaces
- Filesystems' types
- SNMP OIDs
- CPUs and CPU cores (as of version 2.4)

As discovery rules are effectively special kinds of items, you can create your own rules, provided you understand their peculiarity compared to regular items.

You need to create and manage low-level discovery rules in the **Discovery rules** section of a template configuration and not in the usual **Items** section, even if the discovery rules end up creating some kind of items. The main difference between discovered and regular items is that, whereas a regular item usually returns a single value, a discovery item always returns a list, expressed in JSON, of macro value pairs. This list represents all the resources found by the discovery items, together with a means to reference them.

The following table shows Zabbix's supported discovery items and their return values, together with a generalization that should give you an idea of how to create your own rules:

| Discovery item key | Item type | Return values |
|---|---|---|
| `vfs.fs.discovery` | Zabbix agent | `{"data": [`<br>`{"{#FSNAME}":<path>",`<br>`"{#FSTYPE}":"<fstype>"},`<br>`{"{#FSNAME}":<path>",`<br>`"{#FSTYPE}":"<fstype>"},`<br>`{"{#FSNAME}":<path>",`<br>`"{#FSTYPE}":"<fstype>"},`<br>`...`<br>`] }` |
| `net.if.discovery` | Zabbix agent | `{"data":[`<br>`{"{#IFNAME}":"<name>"},`<br>`{"{#IFNAME}":"<name>"},`<br>`{"{#IFNAME}":"<name>"},`<br>`...`<br>`]}` |

| Discovery item key | Item type | Return values |
|---|---|---|
| `snmp.discovery` | SNMP (v1, v2, or v3) agent | `{"data":[`<br>`{"{#SNMPINDEX}":"<idx>",`<br>`"{#SNMPVALUE}":"<value>},`<br>`{"{#SNMPINDEX}":"<idx>",`<br>`"{#SNMPVALUE}":"<value>},`<br>`{"{#SNMPINDEX}":"<idx>",`<br>`"{#SNMPVALUE}":"<value>},`<br>`...`<br>`]}` |
| `system.cpu.discovery` | Zabbix agent | `{"data":[`<br>`{""{#CPU.NUMBER}":"<idx>", "{#CPU.`<br>`STATUS}":"<value>},`<br>`{"{#CPU.NUMBER}":"<idx>", "{#CPU.`<br>`STATUS}":"<value>},`<br>`{"{#CPU.NUMBER}":"<idx>", "{#CPU.`<br>`STATUS}":"<value>},`<br>`...`<br>`]}` |
| `custom.discovery` | Any | `{"data":[`<br>`{"{#CUSTOM1}":"<value>","{#CUSTOM2}`<br>`":"<value>"},`<br>`{"{#CUSTOM1}":"<value>","{#CUSTOM2}`<br>`":"<value>"},`<br>`{"{#CUSTOM1}":"<value>","{#CUSTOM2}`<br>`":"<value>"},`<br>`...`<br>`]}` |

Just as with all SNMP items, the item key is not really important as long as it is unique. It's the SNMP OID value that you ask an agent for that makes the difference: you can create different SNMP discovery rules that look for different kinds of resources by changing the item key and looking for different OID values. The custom discovery example is even more abstract as it will depend on the actual item type.

As you can see, a discovery item always returns a list of values, but the actual contents of the list change, depending on what resources you are looking for. In the case of a filesystem, the returned list will contain values like `{#FSNAME}`:`"/usr"`, `{#FSTYPE}`:`"btrfs"`, and so on for every discovered filesystem. On the other hand, a network discovery rule will return a list of the names of the discovered network interfaces. This is the case for the default SNMP network interfaces template. Let's see in detail how it works.

The template has a discovery rule called **network interfaces**. It looks just like a regular item as it has a name, a type, an update interval, and a key. It's an SNMP type, so it also has an SNMP OID, IF-MIB::ifDescr. This is a discovery rule, so instead of a single value, it will return a list of all the OIDs that are part of the IF-MIB::ifDescr subtree for that particular device. This means that it will return the OID and its value for all the network interfaces present on the device. Every time the discovery rule is executed on a host (based on the update interval, just like any other item), it will return a list of all interfaces that are available at that particular moment. If the device had four network interfaces, it could return something similar to this:

```
{"data" : [
            {  "{#SNMPINDEX}" : "1",
               "{#SNMPVALUE}" : "FastEthernet0/0"},
            {  "{#SNMPINDEX}" : "2",
               "{#SNMPVALUE}" : "FastEthernet0/1"},
            {  "{#SNMPINDEX}" : "3",
               "{#SNMPVALUE}" : "FastEthernet1/0"},
            {  "{#SNMPINDEX}" : "4",
               "{#SNMPVALUE}" : "FastEthernet1/1"},
        ]}
```

The discovery rule will then proceed to apply the list to the item and trigger prototypes it has configured, as follows:

CONFIGURATION OF ITEM PROTOTYPES

**Item prototypes of** Network interfaces

Displaying **1** to **8** of **8** found

« Template list   **Template:** Template SNMP Interfaces   « Discovery list   **Discovery:** Network interfaces   Item prototypes (8)   Trigger prototypes (1)

| Name ↑ | Key | Interval | History | Trends |
|---|---|---|---|---|
| Admin status of interface {#SNMPVALUE} | ifAdminStatus[{#SNMPVALUE}] | 60 | 7 | 365 |
| Alias of interface {#SNMPVALUE} | ifAlias[{#SNMPVALUE}] | 3600 | 7 | |
| Description of interface {#SNMPVALUE} | ifDescr[{#SNMPVALUE}] | 3600 | 7 | |
| Inbound errors on interface {#SNMPVALUE} | ifInErrors[{#SNMPVALUE}] | 60 | 7 | 365 |
| Incoming traffic on interface {#SNMPVALUE} | ifInOctets[{#SNMPVALUE}] | 60 | 7 | 365 |
| Operational status of interface {#SNMPVALUE} | ifOperStatus[{#SNMPVALUE}] | 60 | 7 | 365 |
| Outbound errors on interface {#SNMPVALUE} | ifOutErrors[{#SNMPVALUE}] | 60 | 7 | 365 |
| Outgoing traffic on interface {#SNMPVALUE} | ifOutOctets[{#SNMPVALUE}] | 60 | 7 | 365 |

Taking the **Incoming traffic on interface {#SNMPVALUE}** item prototype as an example, you can see how it all comes together:

| Item prototype | |
|---|---|
| Name | Incoming traffic on interface $1 |
| Type | SNMPv3 agent ▾ |
| Key | ifInOctets[{#SNMPVALUE}] |
| SNMP OID | IF-MIB::ifInOctets.{#SNMPINDEX} |
| Context name | |
| Security name | |
| Security level | noAuthNoPriv ▾ |
| Port | |
| Type of information | Numeric (unsigned) ▾ |
| Data type | Decimal ▾ |
| Units | bps |
| Use custom multiplier | ✔ 8 |
| Update interval (in sec) | 60 |

The `{#SNMPVALUE}` macro is used in the item's key and, therefore, in the item's name as well (look at the $1 macro that references the first argument of the item's key).

On the other hand, the `{#SNMPINDEX}` macro will be used by Zabbix to actually get the incoming traffic value for that specific interface as it should be clear by now if you observe the value in the **SNMP OID** field.

When configuring a template's discovery rules, you don't need to care about the actual values returned in their lists, nor the lists' length. The only thing you have to know is the name of the macros that you can reference in your prototypes. These are to be referenced in the second half of the low-level discovery mechanism, object prototypes. You create them as regular template entities, making sure you use the discovery item macros where needed, and Zabbix will take care of the rest for you, creating for each item prototype as many items as there are elements in the list returned by the discovery rule, for each trigger prototype as many triggers as there are elements in the list returned, and so on.

So, when you apply the template to a host, it will create items, triggers, and graphs based on the resources discovered by the discovery items and configured according to the discovery prototypes.

Custom discovery rules, from this point of view, work exactly in the same way as custom items, whether you decide to use agent-side scripts (thereby using a custom `zabbix.agent` item key), external scripts, database queries, or anything else. The only things you have to make sure of is that your custom items return keys/values that follow the JSON syntax, as shown in the preceding table, and that you reference your custom macros in the entities prototypes that you will create.

Let's see an example of a custom discovery rule using again Nmap and its output to dynamically create some items for a host, representing the open port it has, and the kind of services that are listening. Why would you want to use Nmap and a port scan? The device you need to monitor maybe doesn't support the Zabbix agent, so if you just ask for the output of netstat, you might not be able to install the agent for administrative reasons, or you might have to make sure that the services are also available from another network, so checking them from afar, instead of directly on the host, will enable you to also verify your firewall rules, killing two birds with one stone.

Either way, we'll create an external check item per open TCP port, configured as a character-type item. Each item will contain the name of the service that was found listening, if any, as reported by Nmap's service discovery facilities.

Start by creating the discovery rule as an external check that will call a port-mapping script, as follows:

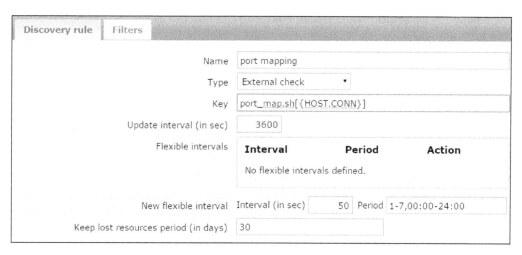

As you can see, the script will receive the host's IP as the only argument, and it will run once an hour for every host that has this discovery rule configured and is active.

The script itself is very simple and is based on NMAP's XML output coupled with the nifty xml2 tool you already used in *Chapter 3, Monitoring Your Network Services,* as follows:

```bash
#!/bin/bash
IPADDR=$1
#store ports as array
PORTS=( $(nmap -sV -oX - ${IPADDR} | xml2 | grep portid | cut -
  d'=' -f2) )
#count elements of the array and use as counter for later
  processing
COUNTER=${#PORTS[@]}

#open JSON
echo '{"data":['
#loop through ports and print key/value
for PORT in "${PORTS[@]}"; do
 COUNTER=$(( COUNTER - 1))
 if [ $COUNTER -ne 0 ]; then
  echo "{\"{#PORTID}\" : \"${PORT}\"}",
 else
  #it's the last element. To have valid JSON We don't add a
    trailing comma
  echo "{\"{#PORTID}\" : \"${PORT}\"}"
 fi
done

#close JSON
echo ]}
#exit with clean exit code
exit 0
```

The line starting with nmap is the heart of the script. The -oX option enables XML output, which is more stable and easy to manage compared to the normal one. The dash after -oX specifies stdout as the output instead of a regular file, so we can pipe the result to xml2 and then take only the lines that contain portid, that is, the open port numbers for that host.

As a result, the script just outputs a simple JSON object. Here's an example of what the discovery rule will get, as shown from the command line:

```
./port_map.sh '127.0.0.1'
```

```
{"data":[
```

```
{"{#PORTID}" : "22"},
{"{#PORTID}" : "25"},
{"{#PORTID}" : "80"},
{"{#PORTID}" : "631"},
{"{#PORTID}" : "3306"}
]}
```

It's now time to define the item and trigger prototypes, based on the open port that you found. We'll show here an example of an item prototype that will return the name and version of the daemon listening on the port, as returned, once again, by Nmap:

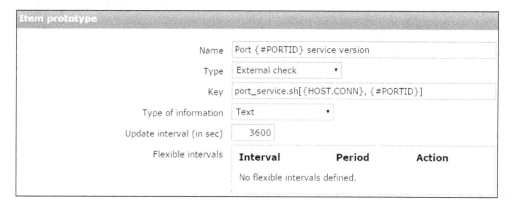

The external check will call a script that is even simpler than the previous one, as follows:

```
#!/bin/bash
IPADDR=$1
PORT=$2
nmap -sV -oX - -p ${PORT} ${IPADDR} | xml2 | grep
    'port/service/@\(product\|version\|extrainfo\)'
```

Compared to the previous Nmap command, we added a -sV option to make NMAP run a series of probes in order to find out what service is running behind that open port and a -p option to specify a single port to scan.

The output was kept simple on purpose to show you an example of xml2's output. You can, of course, slice it and dice it to suit your own needs:

```
./port_service.sh 127.0.0.1 80
/nmaprun/host/ports/port/service/@product=Apache httpd
/nmaprun/host/ports/port/service/@version=2.2.15
/nmaprun/host/ports/port/service/@extrainfo=(CentOS)
```

> The amount of information Nmap will be able to get from a network service depends very much on how much and on what kind of data the service is configured to expose. This might depend on built-in parameters or security considerations on the part of the service owner. Compared to the previous example, your mileage can vary.

This is what will appear as the value of the item once the discovery rule is activated.

# Summary

In this chapter, you learned how to use Zabbix's discovery facilities to automate its configuration as much as possible. It should also be clear to you why it's important to minimize the difference between what is configured in Zabbix and what is actually out there on the wire. Keeping track of everything that can appear or disappear on a busy network can be a fulltime job and one that is better suited to automated monitoring facilities like this one. You now have all the skills needed to actually do it, and you are ready to apply them in your real-world environment.

In the next chapter, we'll wrap things up by showing you how to leverage Zabbix's presentation power to create and manage graphs, dynamic maps, and screens.

# 5
# Visualizing Your Topology with Maps and Graphs

As you probably already know, Zabbix's approach to monitoring is based on separating data gathered from trigger logic and event logging. On the one hand, this means that you are able to reference any measurement, present and past, in your triggers, making them all the more powerful. On the other hand, it also means that you have direct access to all your measurement history for all your items.

While sorting through all of your historical data to look for a specific value can certainly be useful, the real advantage here is to leverage Zabbix's graphing and mapping functionalities to aggregate and visualize data in meaningful ways.

In this chapter, you'll see how to create complex graphs from your items' numerical values, how to automatically draw maps that reflect the current status of your network, and how to bring it all together using screens as a tool to customize monitoring data presentation.

## Creating custom graphs

Basic graphical data representation comes for free for any item that has a numeric data type. You just need to go to **Monitoring | Latest Data**, select the host you are interested in, find the relevant item, and click on **Graph** in the last column on the right-hand side. You'll get a line graph with a time slider that you can use to change the timeframe of the graph itself; widen it to cover a longer amount of time, or shorten it to focus on a specific point in time.

Since Zabbix 2.4, you can also compare different items on the fly with ad hoc graphs. These are a direct extension of simple graphs: from **Monitoring | Latest Data**, you just need to mark the checkbox on the left-hand side of every item that you want to graph and select **Display stacked graph** or **Display graph** from the drop-down menu at the bottom of the page, as follows:

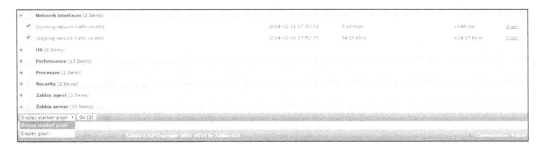

The result is pretty much the one you expect. You also don't have to worry too much about choosing between a normal graph and a stacked graph as you'll be able to switch between the two from the graph itself, as follows:

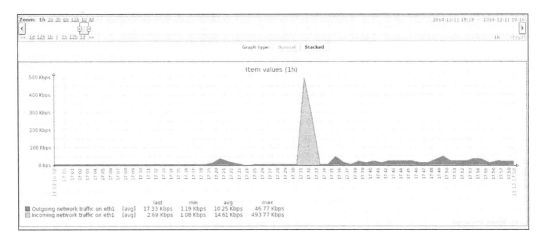

These quick, ad hoc graphs can really cover most of your visualization needs, especially for values that you don't consult that often or if you need to compare items that you normally don't have to, as part of a new analysis or to investigate a new class of problems.

On the other hand, if you need to compare the same types of items over and over, and for different hosts, you'll need a way to *save* your selections so that you are able to access your aggregated graphs without having to specify every time what items need to be graphed. You can achieve all this with custom graphs.

If you like to visualize your percentile data with pie charts, you'll also need to create custom graphs as they're currently the only way to create pie charts in Zabbix.

Custom graphs can be created as part of a host, or better yet as part of a template, or a low-level discovery rule, so that any host inheriting the template or discovery rule will automatically also inherit the custom graph.

To create one, you need to go to **Configuration | Templates**, choose the template you want to put your graph into, select **Graphs**, and click on **Create graph**. This will bring you to the graph creation form. For convenience, the following example will show you some items already added to the item list and some other options already selected instead of an empty form, but you'll easily be able to add your own items by following the add link at the bottom of the item list, as follows:

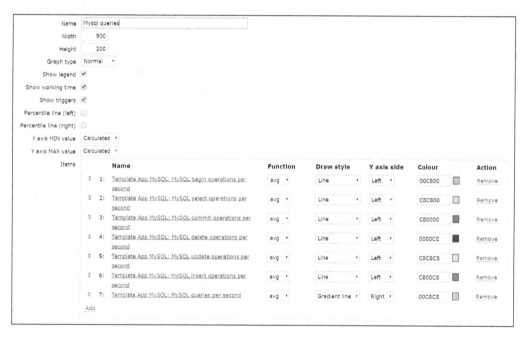

As you can see, there are a few options worth noting. First of all, you can select the graph type between **Normal**, **Stacked**, **Pie**, and **Exploded** (that is, a pie chart with all slices separated instead of close together). Next, if you select the **Show triggers** checkbox, the graph will include a horizontal line for every trigger that has any of the items present in the graph's item list in its expression. You don't have to specify the trigger or find them manually; Zabbix will take care of finding all relevant triggers and show them on the graph.

You can also specify the range of $y$ axis values either as fixed values or calculated based on the data you have. You'll normally want to set them as calculated as this option will usually show the clearest and best-looking graphs, but sometimes, you might want to set them to a fixed value to have a better understanding of how the values change, especially if they fluctuate a lot between very big and very small values, and the item expresses a percentile range.

Moving to the item list, you can order the items by dragging and dropping the blue arrows on the left-hand side of the item's name and change their color by either specifying an RGB value or choosing from a color palette.

The draw style can be quite useful if you want a specific item to stand out from the rest. There are quite a few styles available for a normal graph, while this option is not available for stacked and pie charts.

The **Function** drop-down menu enables you to choose how the item should be graphed for every tick in the $x$ axis: you can choose between the minimum value, the maximum one, and the average. Keep in mind that the $x$-axis tick density will change dynamically with the time scale of the graph (you can select different timeframes while looking at a graph; you don't have to specify them in advance): for timeframes up to an hour, it will show every sample collected, depending on the items' sample frequency; for larger timeframes, you'll have $x$-axis ticks proportional to the timeframe selected, which is a few minutes if the global timeframe is a few hours, to days or weeks if you select months' or years' worth of monitoring data. For every tick, Zabbix will use the function you selected here to plot the item value either by selecting the maximum, the minimum, or the average value for that time tick.

Finally, you can choose whether the $y$ axis for an item will be shown on the left-hand side or the right-hand side. One of the reasons to separate different items on different $y$-axis sides is that maybe you are plotting on the same graph items that have absolute values together with items that express a percentile value. In this case, it makes sense to show the absolute scale on one side and the percentile one on the other side of the graph.

Another reason might be that you are plotting together items that will show, on average, very big or very small values, and you can predict ahead of time the ones that will gravitate towards the bottom of the scale, and the ones that will make the scale go up with big values. In that case, you might want to separate the two; otherwise, the items with big values will make the others look very flat and not very informative on the chart. This is the case illustrated in the preceding graph: we predicted that the total number of queries would be much bigger (by definition) compared to all the others, so we moved its $y$ axis to the right-hand side. Here's the result of the graph we created:

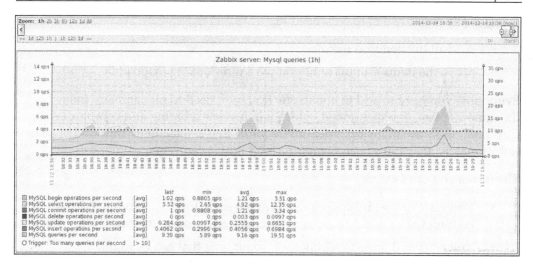

What we haven't shown here, but you can easily imagine, is that as with almost everything in Zabbix, you are not limited to graphing items from the same host: you can just as easily graph the same item from different hosts, or even different items from different hosts. You might be interested, for example, in tracking network traffic from a bunch of different routers and looking at how this traffic changes in time, which machines are the busiest and when, which ones are not as busy as you expected compared to the overall traffic you have, and so on. To do that, you can easily create a graph following the guidelines above, only selecting the relevant network interfaces inbound and outbound items from the different appliances and putting them all on the same item list.

You can use Zabbix's custom graph creation facilities to explore your data in very meaningful ways that can be hard to achieve otherwise: don't be fooled by the fact that it's all mainly time-based (you can't put custom values on the $x$ axis). You'll soon find that the ability to correlate different items from different sources is a very powerful tool for both troubleshooting and capacity planning.

Another powerful tool is Zabbix's mapping facility. We'll explore a few interesting aspects of map creation and maintenance in the following section.

# Maps – a quick setup for a large topology

Creating complex maps is the kind of job that can take a lot of time. While doing a practical example, if you would like to design a map of 20-30 elements, it is easy to spend up to 2 hours even if you already know the job.

To manually produce a map, you need to:

- Add all the items on the map
- Move the items around until you see a nice-looking disposition

Every time you need to add in a map one host, you need to repeat many times the same steps as aforementioned, which will become a boring and complex task. Currently, there are many open-feature requests that can facilitate this kind of task; unfortunately, they have been open for a long time, even years.

The issues you can face are:

- You can't move multiple elements at the same time, something that can be found at `https://support.zabbix.com/browse/ZBXNEXT-161`
- You can't add hosts in a bulk way, something that can be found at `https://support.zabbix.com/browse/ZBXNEXT-163`
- You can't clone any existing map element, something that can be found at `https://support.zabbix.com/browse/ZBXNEXT-51`
- When you are using icons, you can't select them automatically, so you need to check their size and see whether they fit on your map, something that can be found at `https://support.zabbix.com/browse/ZBXNEXT-1608`

For all those issues, we need to find a different way to automate this long and slow process. Clearly, this is the kind of task that needs to be automated as much as possible.

# Maps – automating the DOT creation

What is missing here is something that can process our information and produce as output something usable by Zabbix. To automate this task, there is one library that can help us — **NetworkX** — which is available at `http://networkx.github.io/`.

NetworkX is a Python software library tailor-made for the creation, manipulation, and study of dynamic network structures.

In this example, we assume that you're using Cisco Prime, which is a vendor-specific tool to export a discovered topology.

Anyway, this concept is still valid as here we are going to use an export file obtained, which is in CSV. This kind of CSV can be obtained as an export from many other vendors' software and can be easily produced from any third-party software.

The file that we are going to parse is in the following form:

*IP address, System name, SysObjectID, Found by modules, Neighbors, Status*

As you can see, it contains the IP address of the device discovered, the system name, the OID of the system, the module that found the device, a list of all the neighbors that are connected to it, and it ends with the status.

The following is an example of the line that we are expecting to see:

```
10.12.50.1,main.example.com,.1.3.6.1.4.1.9.1.896,System,"10.12.2.1
  , 10.12.2.2, 10.12.3.1, 10.12.4.1, 10.12.5.1",Reachable
```

We are mostly interested in the following fields:

- IP address
- System name
- SysObjectID
- Neighbors

Then, what we can do is write some Python lines that can read this file, identify all the required information, and write in the output a DOT file.

Here, I am going to spend a few words about the DOT notation, performing an example in order to clarify how this notation is done.

First of all, I would like to explain why we are going to have a Graphviz DOT file.

The Graphviz DOT file is really easy to read, maintain, and update, and nevertheless, it can be stored in a CVS or SVN.

Something that is really important to have is a file that can be quickly used to spot all the differences between versions and is easy to maintain. Also, we are considering using it as it is a standard language and a good starting point, on which we can transform all our acquired data from all the different versions of export.

Indeed, some other vendor-specific software can export the same data but in a different form, so it is important to normalize all our data in a common language.

This common language file will be the file to use to populate our Zabbix map.

This section, as you probably already have understood, will be a large usage of the Graphviz's packages.

The easiest way to install and maintain Graphviz on Red Hat Enterprise Linux is to use the dedicated yum repository. To set up yum, first of all, you need to download the graphviz-rhel.repo file and save it (as root) in /etc/yum.repos.d/, as follows:

```
# cd /etc/yum.repos.d
# wget http://www.graphviz.org/graphviz-rhel.repo
--2014-11-27 02:52:17--  http://www.graphviz.org/graphviz-rhel.repo
Resolving www.graphviz.org... 204.178.9.49
Connecting to www.graphviz.org|204.178.9.49|:80... connected.
HTTP request sent, awaiting response... 200 OK
Length: 1138 (1.1K) [text/plain]
Saving to: "graphviz-rhel.repo"

100%[======================================>] 1,138        --.-K/s    in
0s

2014-11-27 02:52:17 (134 MB/s) - "graphviz-rhel.repo" saved
[1138/1138]

# ls -la graphviz-rhel.repo
-rw-r--r--. 1 root root 1138 Feb 16  2012 graphviz-rhel.repo
```

Then, you can finally list all the Graphviz packages as root:

**yum list available 'graphviz*'**

Install them, as follows:

**yum install 'graphviz*'**

Now that we've clarified the reason why we're doing those steps, it is important to walk through the DOT language. The DOT language is a language made to represent objects connected between each other.

While performing a practical example, if we want to define two connected nodes with the Graphviz DOT language, we can do as follows:

```
graph {
A -- B
}
```

This is a very easy-to-understand language; we are now representing two nodes connected to each other.

To see the graphical result, we can use a simple Python program xdot.py available for download here:

```
https://github.com/jrfonseca/xdot.py
```

All you have to do is download the program, write a file with the Graphviz DOT content that we showed previously, and then run the program, as follows:

```
xdot.py example.dot
```

The result is the DOT expressed topology visualized, as follows:

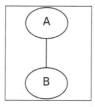

Using the same grammar, we can define three nodes connected, as follows:

```
graph {
A -- B -- C
}
```

Using the same xdot.py used previously, the result is the following:

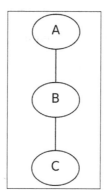

Writing a couple of lines more, we can even avoid using long names using the following grammar:

```
graph {
   //We can create aliases to avoid to use very long names on the
      dependency definition
   Andrea [hostname="andrea.dalle.vacche.example.com"]
   Stefano [hostname="stefano.kewan.lee.example.com"]
   router [label="Our network router" zbximage="router"]
   //now it's time to define connections between the nodes
```

```
        //This notation allows for multiple edges from "router" in one
          go
        router -- { Andrea Stefano }
    }
```

And the result is shown here:

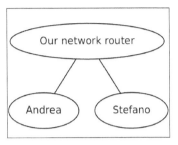

For a detailed documentation of this grammar, please refer to the official documentation available at http://www.graphviz.org/content/dot-language.

Until now, we've covered all that is needed to know for our small application.

Now, we can come back to our CSV file we extracted from Cisco Prime.

Here is the CSV of a very simple network, but it can be applied on very complex network topologies, as well:

```
[root@localhost graphs]# cat my_export.csv
IP Address,System Name,SysObjectID,Found By Modules,Neighbors,Status
10.12.20.1,main.example.com,.1.3.6.1.4.1.9.1.896,System,"10.12.2.1,
10.12.2.2, 10.12.3.1, 10.12.4.1, 10.12.5.1",Reachable
10.12.2.1,cluster1.example.com,.1.3.6.1.4.1.9.1.634,System,"10.12.2.2,
192.168.99.1",Reachable
10.12.1.1,london.example.com,.1.3.6.1.4.1.9.1.503,System,"",Reachable
10.12.2.2,cluster2.example.com,.1.3.6.1.4.1.9.1.634,System,"10.12.2.1,
192.168.99.1",Reachable
10.12.3.1,switch1.example.com,.1.3.6.1.4.1.9.1.503,System,"192.168.99
.1",Reachable
10.12.4.1,4.example.com,.1.3.6.1.4.1.9.1.502,System,"192.168.99.1,
10.12.4.42, 10.12.4.47, 10.12.4.48, 10.12.4.49",Reachable
10.12.4.45,4d.example.com,.1.3.6.1.4.1.9.1.503,System,"10.12.4.1",Rea
chable
10.12.4.46,4e.example.com,.1.3.6.1.4.1.9.1.502,System,"10.12.4.1",Rea
chable
```

```
10.12.4.47,4f.example.com,.1.3.6.1.4.1.9.1.503,System,"10.12.4.1",Rea
chable
10.12.4.48,4g.example.com,.1.3.6.1.4.1.9.1.503,System,"10.12.4.1",Rea
chable
10.12.5.1,5.example.com,.1.3.6.1.4.1.9.1.502,System,"192.168.99.1,
10.12.5.45, 10.12.5.43, 10.12.5.44, 10.12.5.46, 10.12.5.47,
10.12.5.48,  10.12.6.1",Reachable
10.12.5.44,5c.example.com,.1.3.6.1.4.1.9.1.503,System,"10.12.5.1",Rea
chable
10.12.5.45,5d.example.com,.1.3.6.1.4.1.9.1.503,System,"10.12.5.1",Rea
chable
10.12.5.46,5e.example.com,.1.3.6.1.4.1.9.1.502,System,"10.12.5.1",Rea
chable
10.12.5.47,5f.example.com,.1.3.6.1.4.1.9.1.503,System,"10.12.5.1",Rea
chable
10.12.5.48,5g.example.com,.1.3.6.1.4.1.9.1.503,System,"10.12.5.1",Rea
chable
10.12.5.155,5i.example.com,.1.3.6.1.4.1.9.1.634,System,"10.12.5.1",Re
achable
10.12.6.1,6.example.com,.1.3.6.1.4.1.9.1.502,System," 10.12.6.45,
10.12.6.46, 10.12.6.47, , 10.12.5.1",Reachable
10.12.6.45,6d.example.com,.1.3.6.1.4.1.9.1.503,System,"10.12.6.1",Rea
chable
10.12.6.46,6e.example.com,.1.3.6.1.4.1.9.1.502,System,"10.12.6.1",Rea
chable
10.12.6.47,6f.example.com,.1.3.6.1.4.1.9.1.503,System,"10.12.6.1",Rea
chable
```

From this file, we see that all the relations between neighbors are already contained in the CSV, and that we only need to convert them into DOT notation using the node notation.

Here, we can start coding a few Python lines to produce our desired output:

```
#First of all we need to import csv and Networkx
import csv
import networkx as nx
#Then we need to define who is our zabbix server and some other detail
to properly produce the DOT file
zabbix_service_ipaddr = "192.168.1.100"
main_loop_ipaddr = "10.12.20.1"
main_vlan_ipaddr = "149.148.56.1"

# Now we can finally create our graph
G=nx.Graph()
```

```
# we can open our CSV file
csv_reader = csv.DictReader( open( 'my_export.csv' ), \
    delimiter=",", \
    fieldnames=( "ipaddress", "hostname", "oid", "dontcare",
"neighbors" ))
# Skip the header
csv_reader.next()

for row in csv_reader:
    neighbor_list = row["neighbors"].split( "," )

    for neighbor in neighbor_list:
        # Remove spaces
        neighbor = neighbor.lstrip()

  # Add neighbors,and here we've decided to ignore isolated nodes
        if neighbor != "":
            G.add_edge( row["ipaddress"], neighbor )

            # Add additional information to nodes or edges here
            G.node[row["ipaddress"]]["hostname"] = row["hostname"]
# Cisco Prime doesn't export all IP addresses of a device
# but only the first for each network, Here we merge hosts with
# multiple IP addresses
mapping = {main_vlan_ipaddr: main_loop_ipaddr}
G = nx.relabel_nodes( G, mapping )

# Remove cluster connection not needed in our map
G.remove_edge( "10.12.2.1", "10.12.2.2" )

# Adding connection between Zabbix server and main switch
G.add_edge( zabbix_service_ipaddr, main_loop_ipaddr )
main_neigh_list = G.neighbors( main_loop_ipaddr )
# finally write out our file
nx.draw_graphviz( G )
nx.write_dot( G, "/tmp/total.dot" )
```

Now, if you run this small software against the CSV file we have shown before you see our DOT file generated on /tmp/total.dot. Now, it is interesting to see how our DOT file is represented on XDot. Here, in the next diagram, we see the representation of our DOT file:

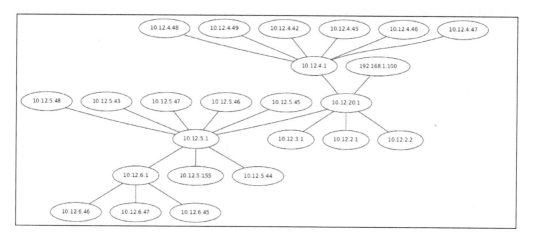

Now, all that we have to do is produce the map starting from the DOT file we just generated.

# Drafting Zabbix maps from DOT

Having arrived at this point, we have our Graphviz DOT file that is waiting to be used. As you can see from the previous image, thanks to Graphviz, we already have a ready-to-go image to use. Then, all we need to do is:

1. Read out the DOT file.
2. Generate the topology using Graphviz.
3. Acquire all the coordinates from our topology generated.
4. Use pyzabbix to connect to our Zabbix server.
5. Generate our topology in a fully automated way.

It's now time to write some lines of Python; the following example is similar to something presented by Volker Fröhlich. Anyway, the code here has been changed and fixed (it did not work well with Zabbix 2.4).

As the first thing, we need to import the ZabbixApi and networkX libraries:

```
import networkx as nx
from pyzabbix import ZabbixAPI
```

Then, we can define the Graphviz DOT file to use as a source; a good example is the one we just generated:

```
dot_file="/tmp/total.dot"
```

In the next few lines, we define our username, password, map dimension, and relative map name:

```
username="Admin"
password="zabbix"
width = 800
height = 600
mapname = "my_network"
```

What follows is a static map to define the element type:

```
ELEMENT_TYPE_HOST = 0
ELEMENT_TYPE_MAP = 1
ELEMENT_TYPE_TRIGGER = 2
ELEMENT_TYPE_HOSTGROUP = 3
ELEMENT_TYPE_IMAGE = 4
ADVANCED_LABELS = 1
LABEL_TYPE_LABEL = 0
```

Then, we can define the icons to use and the relative color code:

```
icons = {
  "router": 23,
  "cloud": 26,
  "desktop": 27,
  "laptop": 28,
  "server": 29,
  "sat": 30,
  "tux": 31,
  "default": 40,
}
colors = {
  "purple": "FF00FF",
  "green": "00FF00",
  "default": "00FF00",
}
```

Now, we define some functions that we can reuse. The first one is to manage the login, and the second one is to define a host lookup, as follows:

```
def api_connect():
  zapi = ZabbixAPI("http://127.0.0.1/zabbix/")
```

```
    zapi.login(username, password)
    return zapi

def host_lookup(hostname):
    hostid = zapi.host.get({"filter": {"host": hostname}})
    if hostid:
        return str(hostid[0]['hostid'])
```

The next thing to do, is read our DOT file and start converting it into a graph:

```
G=nx.read_dot(dot_file)
```

Then, we can finally open our graph, as follows:

```
pos = nx.graphviz_layout(G)
```

> Here, you can select your preferred algorithm. Graphviz supports
> many different kinds of layout, and then you can change the look
> and feel of your map as you prefer. For more information about
> Graphviz, please check the official documentation available at
> http://www.graphviz.org/.

Then, as the graph is already generated, the next thing to do is find the maximum
coordinates of the layout. This will enable us to scale better our predefined map
output size.

```
positionlist=list(pos.values())
maxpos=map(max, zip(*positionlist))
for host, coordinates in pos.iteritems():
    pos[host] = [int(coordinates[0]*width/maxpos[0]*0.95-
coordinates[0]*0.1), int((height-coordinates[1]*height/maxpos[1])*0.95
+coordinates[1]*0.1)]
nx.set_node_attributes(G,'coordinates',pos)
```

> Graphviz and Zabbix use two different data origins: Graphviz
> starts from the bottom-left corner, and Zabbix works starting
> from the top-left corner.

Then, we need to retrieve the `selementids` as they are required for links and even
for the node data coordinates, as follows:

```
selementids = dict(enumerate(G.nodes_iter(), start=1))
selementids = dict((v,k) for k,v in selementids.iteritems())
nx.set_node_attributes(G,'selementid',selementids)
nx.set_node_attributes(G,'selementid',selementids)
```

Now, we define the map on Zabbix, the name, and the relative map size:

```
map_params = {
  "name": mapname,
  "label_type": 0,
  "width": width,
  "height": height
}
element_params=[]
link_params=[]
```

Finally, we can connect to our Zabbix server:

```
zapi = api_connect()
```

Then, prepare all the node information and the coordinates and then set the icon to use, as follows:

```
for node, data in G.nodes_iter(data=True):
  # Generic part
  map_element = {}
  map_element.update({
    "selementid": data['selementid'],
    "x": data['coordinates'][0],
    "y": data['coordinates'][1],
    "use_iconmap": 0,
  })
```

Check whether we have the hostname, as follows:

```
  if "hostname" in data:
    map_element.update({
      "elementtype": ELEMENT_TYPE_HOST,
      "elementid": host_lookup(data['hostname'].strip('"')),
      "iconid_off": icons['server'],
    })
  else:
    map_element.update({
      "elementtype": ELEMENT_TYPE_IMAGE,
      "elementid": 0,
    })
```

We set labels for images, as follows:

```
  if "label" in data:
    map_element.update({
      "label": data['label'].strip('"')
```

```
        })
    if "zbximage" in data:
      map_element.update({
        "iconid_off": icons[data['zbximage'].strip('"')],
      })
    elif "hostname" not in data and "zbximage" not in data:
      map_element.update({
        "iconid_off": icons['default'],
      })

    element_params.append(map_element)
```

Now, we need to scan all the edges to create the element links based on the element we identified, as follows:

```
nodenum = nx.get_node_attributes(G, 'selementid')
for nodea, nodeb, data in G.edges_iter(data=True):
  link = {}
  link.update({
    "selementid1": nodenum[nodea],
    "selementid2": nerodenum[nodeb],
  })

  if "color" in data:
    color =  colors[data['color'].strip('"')]
      link.update({
        "color": color
      })
  else:
    link.update({
      "color": colors['default']
    })

  if "label" in data:
    label =  data['label'].strip('"')
    link.update({
      "label": label,
    })

    link_params.append(link)

# Join the prepared information
map_params["selements"] = element_params
map_params["links"] = link_params
```

Now, we have populated all `map_params`, and now we need to call Zabbix's API with this data:

```
map=zapi.map.create(map_params)
```

The program is now complete, and we can let it run! In a real-world case, the time spent to design a topology of more than 2,500 hosts is only 2–3 seconds!

We can test the software here, proposed against the DOT file we generated before:

```
[root@localhost]# time ./Generate_MyMap.py
real    0m0.005s
user    0m0.002s
sys     0m0.003s
```

As you can see, our software is really quick… but let's check what has been generated. In the next screenshot, you can see the map that is generated automatically in `0.005` seconds:

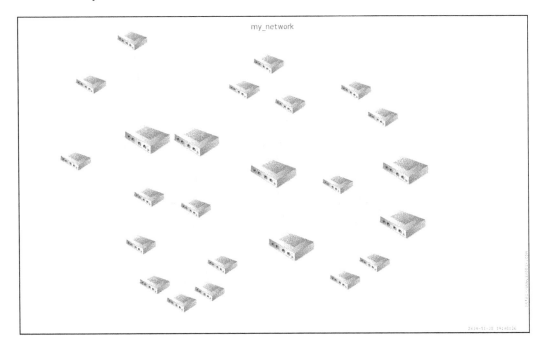

# Putting everything together with screens

Unlike any other Zabbix feature we described in this chapter, screens don't actually give you new or improved information about your monitored data. Pretty much anything that you can decide to put on a **screen** can be found somewhere else in Zabbix.

From maps and graphs, to trigger status and item data, all of this and more can be easily found by exploring the **Monitoring** tab of the web frontend.

But the point of gathering existing data on a Zabbix **screen** is precisely that you bring together related data, or different views of the same data so that you don't have to look for it around the frontend, and so that you can have a good overview of the status of your systems and see at a glance whether there are any problems within your infrastructure.

When you create a screen (**Configuration | Screens | Create screen**), you give it a name and a starting number of rows and columns. Don't worry too much about how many rows and columns you assign to a screen as you will be able to change them during screen configuration.

Once you have the screen created, you can go ahead and configure it by selecting its name in **Configuration | Screens**.

A screen is basically a table with rows and columns that identifies cells. Every cell can contain different types of data:

| Cell type | Description |
| --- | --- |
| Action log | This shows a log of the latest actions executed by Zabbix. You can configure how many actions you want to see in the cell. |
| Clock | This shows an analog clock with the current time. |
| Data overview | This shows the latest item data for a specific group of hosts. |
| Graph | This shows an existing custom graph. |
| Graph prototype | This shows a custom graph created from a low-level discovery rule prototype. |
| History of events | This shows a log of the latest events (these don't necessarily lead to actions). You can configure how many events you want to see in the cell. |
| Host group issues | This shows the current issues for a specific host group. |
| Host issues | This shows the current issues for a specific host. |
| Host's info | This shows a summary of host availability for a specific group, such as the one you find in **Monitoring | Overview**. |
| Map | This shows an existing map. |

| Cell type | Description |
|---|---|
| Plain text | This shows the plain text history of a specific item together with the timestamp for each measurement. You can configure how many entries you want to see in the cell. |
| Screen | This shows an existing screen. Yes, you can embed a screen into another screen if you want. |
| Server info | This shows a summary of the monitoring status for the Zabbix server, such as DB connectivity, number of hosts, items and triggers, new values per second, and so on. |
| Simple graph | This shows the graph for a single item, such as the ones you can see in **Latest data** without creating a custom graph. |
| Simple graph prototype | This is like a simple graph, but is for items created automatically from a low-level discovery rule prototype. |
| System status | This shows a summary of the current issues, divided into host groups and severity. |
| Trigger information | This shows a summary of triggers currently in a problem state, divided by severity. You have to specify a host group. |
| Trigger overview | This shows every trigger status for every host in a specific host group (and optionally, application). |
| URL | This shows the content of an arbitrary web page, given its URL. |

Every cell is also independent from the others: you can bring together data belonging to the same host as well as belonging to different hosts and hosts' groups, depending on how you want to organize your screen.

Finally, for every cell, you can specify how many rows and columns it should span, and for graphic cell types (maps, graphs, and so on), you can also define how much space they should take by specifying the width and height in pixels.

All this flexibility is certainly powerful but can be a bit overwhelming, so here are some general guidelines that you can refer to when you create your own screens.

A very useful type of screen brings together data from a single host so that you can see at a glance its overall performance. You'll typically want to see some graphs in a screen like this, such as network and CPU performance, disk usage, and any application-specific graph or item summary you might need, such as database performance graphs, application server statistics, and so on.

In the following example, we've kept things simple due to space constraints, but you can see how even four graphs can prove useful when put together this way:

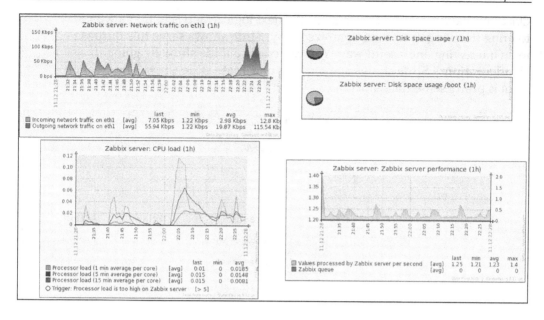

An interesting feature of screen cells is that you can make the content dynamic by flagging the aptly named checkbox. Dynamic cells will refer the same type of content to different hosts depending on the context.

This means that you can create a screen at the template level, flag all cells as dynamic, and just like that, every host inheriting the template will also inherit a personalized screen, with all graphs and tables referencing the aforesaid host. This way, you won't have to manually create a specific screen for every host.

In another type of screen, you might want to focus on group triggers and issues. In this kind of screen, a typical cell's contents will be some maps, with hosts and links that change color based on trigger status, some **trigger information** and **trigger overview** cells, and possibly a log of the latest events and actions.

Finally, you might want to create specific screens that bring together historical data from different items, such as application-specific log files, output from external commands, such as Nmap, Windows update status for a host, and so on. As usual, the sky's the limit here.

 Keep in mind that the preceding screen types are merely examples that barely scratch the surface of what's possible with Zabbix's screen. You are by no means limited to these types; on the contrary, you are encouraged to mix and match the different cells to suit your own needs. Don't let us stop you from creating awesome screens!

Once you have created a few screens, the next logical step is to find a way to bring them together in an organized way. **Slide shows** serve this purpose in an interesting and useful way. You can create a **slide show** by going to **Configuration | Slide shows** and clicking on **Create slide show**. The creation form is pretty self-explanatory:

| CONFIGURATION OF SLIDE SHOWS | | | |
| --- | --- | --- | --- |
| **Slide** | | | |
| Name | | | |
| Default delay (in seconds) | 30 | | |
| Slides | **Screen** | **Delay** | **Action** |
| | ⬍ 1  Zabbix server | default | Remove |
| | ⬍ 2  router issues | 40 | Remove |
| | Add | | |
| | Add   Cancel | | |

Much like adding items to a custom graph, by clicking on the **Add** link at the bottom of the **Slides** list, you can add existing screens to the slide show, and you can reorder them by dragging and dropping the blue arrows near the screen name in the list. The result will be, quite predictably, a slide show of all the screens you have put in the list. It will run over and over cycling through all the elements. Each slide will have the focus for the number of seconds equal to the default delay if you don't specify anything in the slide's **Delay** field.

Slide shows are very useful when shown on a big screen in a datacenter, but you need to be careful when creating screens that you know will end up in a slide show. Slides don't scroll vertically, so if a screen is bigger than the browser window used to show the slides, you'll never be able to see some of the data. A possible workaround is to create screens that will take up the whole window size, but nothing more. This way, you'll be sure that all relevant data will always show up on the slide show that you play on that big screen you put on the wall for monitoring purposes.

Another workaround is to make sure that for each screen bigger than the window size, you put all important data at the top of the screen. This way, some of the screen's data will show up on the slides, while you'll still be able to access all of it when accessing the screen on its own and not as part of the slideshow.

# Summary

In this chapter, you explored Zabbix's visualization features and learned how to use them to get the most out of your monitoring data. Sometimes, the value of a measurement doesn't lie in the events and actions that it can trigger, but in its correlation with other measurements, both in time (graphs) and instantly (maps). This is especially true with network monitoring, where the ability to predict the future needs of a network, and adapt to them, is just as important as acting on contingent issues.

We have reached the end of our brief journey through Zabbix's configuration and use. Now, you should be able to correctly size a Zabbix installation based on you environment; find the best and most appropriate tools and protocols to monitor your data; automate device discovery and monitoring as much as possible (and when not to automate it); and move beyond actions and triggers and visualize all your data in meaningful ways.

With all these skills under your belt, we are confident that you'll be able to adapt a powerful and flexible tool like Zabbix to your own network and not be confined to default templates that may, or may not, reflect your actual monitoring needs.

Monitoring a computer network is often also a discovery journey, where you can gain unexpected wisdom from apparently dry and uninspiring data, such as SNMP values and server logs. With this short book, we hope we have shown you how Zabbix can be an excellent means to gain such wisdom if you are willing to play with it for a while and put to good use all its powerful features.

# Partitioning the Zabbix Database

## MySQL partitioning

Here are all the stored procedures you need to create to properly handle database partitioning with MySQL.

You need to create all of them in your Zabbix database.

Note that all the procedures described here are also available at `https://github.com/smartmarmot/zabbix_network_monitoring/Chapter1`.

## The partition_maintenance procedure

This is the most important procedure, which will manage all the other stored procedures involved in the creation/drop and verification of partitions, as follows:

```
DELIMITER $$
CREATE PROCEDURE `partition_maintenance`(SCHEMA_NAME VARCHAR(32),
TABLE_NAME VARCHAR(32), KEEP_DATA_DAYS INT, HOURLY_INTERVAL INT,
CREATE_NEXT_INTERVALS INT)
BEGIN
        DECLARE OLDER_THAN_PARTITION_DATE VARCHAR(16);
        DECLARE PARTITION_NAME VARCHAR(16);
        DECLARE LESS_THAN_TIMESTAMP INT;
        DECLARE CUR_TIME INT;

        CALL partition_verify(SCHEMA_NAME, TABLE_NAME, HOURLY_
INTERVAL);
```

```
        SET CUR_TIME = UNIX_TIMESTAMP(DATE_FORMAT(NOW(), '%Y-%m-%d
00:00:00'));
        IF DATE(NOW()) = '2014-04-01' THEN
                SET CUR_TIME = UNIX_TIMESTAMP(DATE_FORMAT(DATE_
ADD(NOW(), INTERVAL 1 DAY), '%Y-%m-%d 00:00:00'));
        END IF;
        SET @__interval = 1;
        create_loop: LOOP
                IF @__interval > CREATE_NEXT_INTERVALS THEN
                        LEAVE create_loop;
                END IF;

                SET LESS_THAN_TIMESTAMP = CUR_TIME + (HOURLY_INTERVAL
* @__interval * 3600);
                SET PARTITION_NAME = FROM_UNIXTIME(CUR_TIME + HOURLY_
INTERVAL * (@__interval - 1) * 3600, 'p%Y%m%d%H00');
                CALL partition_create(SCHEMA_NAME, TABLE_NAME,
PARTITION_NAME, LESS_THAN_TIMESTAMP);
                SET @__interval=@__interval+1;
        END LOOP;

        SET OLDER_THAN_PARTITION_DATE=DATE_FORMAT(DATE_SUB(NOW(),
INTERVAL KEEP_DATA_DAYS DAY), '%Y%m%d0000');
        CALL partition_drop(SCHEMA_NAME, TABLE_NAME, OLDER_THAN_
PARTITION_DATE);

END$$
DELIMITER ;
```

This stored procedure will be the core of our housekeeping. It will be called with the following syntax:

```
CALL partition_maintenance('<zabbix_db_name>', '<table_name>', <days_
to_keep_data>, <hourly_interval>, <num_future_intervals_to_create>)
```

# The partition_create procedure

This procedure is responsible for creating new partitions across your schema. What follows here is the procedure itself:

```
DELIMITER $$
CREATE PROCEDURE `partition_create`(SCHEMANAME VARCHAR(64), TABLENAME
VARCHAR(64), PARTITIONNAME VARCHAR(64), CLOCK INT)
BEGIN
        /*
                SCHEMANAME = The DB schema in which to make changes
```

```
            TABLENAME = The table with partitions to potentially delete
            PARTITIONNAME = The name of the partition to create
    */
    /*
        Verify that the partition does not already exist
    */

    DECLARE RETROWS INT;
    SELECT COUNT(1) INTO RETROWS
    FROM information_schema.partitions
    WHERE table_schema = SCHEMANAME AND TABLE_NAME = TABLENAME AND
partition_name = PARTITIONNAME;

    IF RETROWS = 0 THEN
            /*
                1. Print a message indicating that a partition was
created.
                2. Create the SQL to create the partition.
                3. Execute the SQL from #2.
            */
            SELECT CONCAT( "partition_create(", SCHEMANAME, ",",
TABLENAME, ",", PARTITIONNAME, ",", CLOCK, ")" ) AS msg;
            SET @SQL = CONCAT( 'ALTER TABLE ', SCHEMANAME, '.',
TABLENAME, ' ADD PARTITION (PARTITION ', PARTITIONNAME, ' VALUES LESS
THAN (', CLOCK, '));' );
            PREPARE STMT FROM @SQL;
            EXECUTE STMT;
            DEALLOCATE PREPARE STMT;
        END IF;
END$$
DELIMITER ;
```

# The partition_verify procedure

This partition is responsible for verifying whether a partition is already present, and if it isn't, partition_verify will create them, as follows:

```
DELIMITER $$
CREATE PROCEDURE `partition_verify`(SCHEMANAME VARCHAR(64), TABLENAME
VARCHAR(64), HOURLYINTERVAL INT(11))
BEGIN
        DECLARE PARTITION_NAME VARCHAR(16);
        DECLARE RETROWS INT(11);
        DECLARE FUTURE_TIMESTAMP TIMESTAMP;
```

```
        /*
         * Check if any partitions exist for the given SCHEMANAME.
TABLENAME.
         */
        SELECT COUNT(1) INTO RETROWS
        FROM information_schema.partitions
        WHERE table_schema = SCHEMANAME AND TABLE_NAME = TABLENAME AND
partition_name IS NULL;

        /*
         * If partitions do not exist, go ahead and partition the
table
         */
        IF RETROWS = 1 THEN
                /*
                 * Take the current date at 00:00:00 and add
HOURLYINTERVAL to it.  This is the timestamp below which we will store
values.
                 * We begin partitioning based on the beginning of a
day.  This is because we don't want to generate a random partition
                 * that won't necessarily fall in line with the
desired partition naming (ie: if the hour interval is 24 hours, we
could
                 * end up creating a partition now named
"p201403270600" when all other partitions will be like
"p201403280000").
                 */
                SET FUTURE_TIMESTAMP = TIMESTAMPADD(HOUR,
HOURLYINTERVAL, CONCAT(CURDATE(), " ", '00:00:00'));
                SET PARTITION_NAME = DATE_FORMAT(CURDATE(),
'p%Y%m%d%H00');

                -- Create the partitioning query
                SET @__PARTITION_SQL = CONCAT("ALTER TABLE ",
SCHEMANAME, ".", TABLENAME, " PARTITION BY RANGE(`clock`)");
                SET @__PARTITION_SQL = CONCAT(@__PARTITION_SQL,
"(PARTITION ", PARTITION_NAME, " VALUES LESS THAN (", UNIX_
TIMESTAMP(FUTURE_TIMESTAMP), "));");

                -- Run the partitioning query
                PREPARE STMT FROM @__PARTITION_SQL;
                EXECUTE STMT;
                DEALLOCATE PREPARE STMT;
        END IF;
END$$
DELIMITER ;
```

# The partition_drop procedure

This stored procedure is responsible for dropping the partitions older than a given period, as follows:

```
DELIMITER $$
CREATE PROCEDURE `partition_drop`(SCHEMANAME VARCHAR(64), TABLENAME
VARCHAR(64), DELETE_BELOW_PARTITION_DATE BIGINT)
BEGIN
        /*
            SCHEMANAME = The DB schema in which to make changes
            TABLENAME = The table with partitions to potentially delete
            DELETE_BELOW_PARTITION_DATE = Delete any partitions with
names that are dates older than this one (yyyy-mm-dd)
        */
        DECLARE done INT DEFAULT FALSE;
        DECLARE drop_part_name VARCHAR(16);

        /*
            Get a list of all the partitions that are older than the
date
            in DELETE_BELOW_PARTITION_DATE.  All partitions are
prefixed with
            a "p", so use SUBSTRING TO get rid of that character.
        */
        DECLARE myCursor CURSOR FOR
                SELECT partition_name
                FROM information_schema.partitions
                WHERE table_schema = SCHEMANAME AND TABLE_NAME =
TABLENAME AND CAST(SUBSTRING(partition_name FROM 2) AS UNSIGNED) <
DELETE_BELOW_PARTITION_DATE;
        DECLARE CONTINUE HANDLER FOR NOT FOUND SET done = TRUE;

        /*
            Create the basics for when we need to drop the partition.
Also, create
            @drop_partitions to hold a comma-delimited list of all
partitions that
            should be deleted.
        */
        SET @alter_header = CONCAT("ALTER TABLE ", SCHEMANAME, ".",
TABLENAME, " DROP PARTITION ");
        SET @drop_partitions = "";
```

```
        /*
            Start looping through all the partitions that are too old.
        */
        OPEN myCursor;
        read_loop: LOOP
                FETCH myCursor INTO drop_part_name;
                IF done THEN
                        LEAVE read_loop;
                END IF;
                SET @drop_partitions = IF(@drop_partitions = "", drop_
part_name, CONCAT(@drop_partitions, ",", drop_part_name));
        END LOOP;
        IF @drop_partitions != "" THEN
                /*
                    1. Build the SQL to drop all the necessary
partitions.
                    2. Run the SQL to drop the partitions.
                    3. Print out the table partitions that were
deleted.
                */
                SET @full_sql = CONCAT(@alter_header, @drop_
partitions, ";");
                PREPARE STMT FROM @full_sql;
                EXECUTE STMT;
                DEALLOCATE PREPARE STMT;

                SELECT CONCAT(SCHEMANAME, ".", TABLENAME) AS `table`,
@drop_partitions AS `partitions_deleted`;
        ELSE
                /*
                    No partitions are being deleted, so print out "N/A"
(Not applicable) to indicate
                    that no changes were made.
                */
                SELECT CONCAT(SCHEMANAME, ".", TABLENAME) AS `table`,
"N/A" AS `partitions_deleted`;
        END IF;
END$$
DELIMITER;
```

# The partition_maintenance_all procedure

This procedure calls the `partition_maintenance` procedure for each history/trend table. Please note that for all the history tables, we are applying the same intervals, which are 730 days of trend data and 28 days of history data. Here's how this procedure works:

```
DELIMITER $$
CREATE PROCEDURE `partition_maintenance_all`(SCHEMA_NAME VARCHAR(32))
BEGIN
            CALL partition_maintenance(SCHEMA_NAME, 'history', 28,
24, 14);
            CALL partition_maintenance(SCHEMA_NAME, 'history_log',
28, 24, 14);
            CALL partition_maintenance(SCHEMA_NAME, 'history_str',
28, 24, 14);
            CALL partition_maintenance(SCHEMA_NAME, 'history_
text', 28, 24, 14);
            CALL partition_maintenance(SCHEMA_NAME, 'history_
uint', 28, 24, 14);
            CALL partition_maintenance(SCHEMA_NAME, 'trends', 730,
24, 14);
            CALL partition_maintenance(SCHEMA_NAME, 'trends_uint',
730, 24, 14);
END$$
DELIMITER;
```

# Housekeeping configuration

As per our example, the housekeeping needs to be configured, as shown in the following screenshot, with a history data storage period of 730 days and a trend data storage period of 28 days. Here, you can change those values bearing in mind that you also need to change the parameter passed to the stored procedures.

To change the housekeeping setting in the web interface, you simply need to go to **Administration | General | Housekeeping** (from the drop-down list), and here is the configuration:

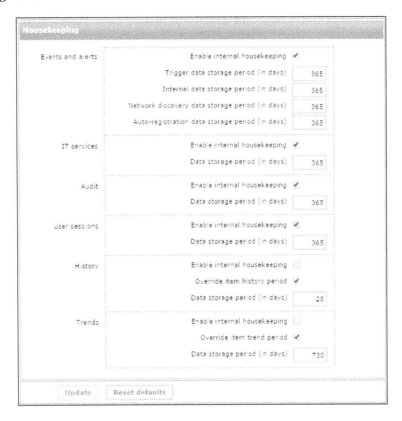

# B
# Collecting Squid Metrics

## Squid metric script

Here, you can find the script we discussed in *Chapter 3, Monitoring Your Network Services,* and create the script in the usual location, that is, at /home/zabbix/bin/ squidcheck.sh.

Create the script with the following content:

```
cat squidcheck.sh
#!/bin/bash
VERSION="1.0"

function usage()
{
  echo "squidcheck   version: $VERSION"
  echo "usage:"
  echo "  $0 http_requests          - Number of HTTP requests
received"
  echo "  $0 clients                - Number of clients accessing
cache"
  echo "  $0 icp_received           - Number of ICP messages
received"
  echo "  $0 icp_sent               - Number of ICP messages sent"
  echo "  $0 icp_queued             - Number of queued ICP
replies"
  echo "  $0 htcp_received          - Number of HTCP messages
received"
  echo "  $0 htcp_sent              - Number of HTCP messages
sent"
  echo "  $0 req_fail_ratio         - Request failure ratio"
```

```
    echo "  $0 avg_http_req_per_min         - Average HTTP requests per
minute since start"
    echo "  $0 avg_icp_msg_per_min          - Average ICP messages per
minute since start"
    echo "  $0 request_hit_ratio            - Request Hit Ratios"
    echo "  $0 byte_hit_ratio_5             - Byte Hit Ratio 5 mins"
    echo "  $0 byte_hit_ratio_60            - Byte Hit Ratio 60 mins"
    echo "  $0 request_mem_hit_ratio_5       - Request Memory Hit Ratios 5
mins"
    echo "  $0 request_mem_hit_ratio_60      - Request Memory Hit Ratios 60
mins"
    echo "  $0 request_disk_hit_ratio_5      - Request Disk Hit Ratios 5
mins"
    echo "  $0 request_disk_hit_ratio_60     - Request Disk Hit Ratios 60
mins"
    echo "  $0 servicetime_httpreq          - HTTP Requests (All)"
    echo "  $0 process_mem                  - Process Data Segment Size
via sbrk"
    echo "  $0 cpu_usage                    - CPU Usage"
    echo "  $0 cache_size_disk              - Storage Swap size"
    echo "  $0 cache_size_mem               - Storage Mem size"
    echo "  $0 mean_obj_size                - Mean Object Size"
    echo "  $0 filedescr_max                - Maximum number of file
descriptors"
    echo "  $0 filedescr_avail              - Available number of file
descriptors"
}


########
# Main #
########


if [[ $# !=  1 ]];then
        #No Parameter
        usage
        exit 0
fi
case $1 in
"http_requests")
    value="`squidclient mgr:info|grep 'Number of HTTP requests
received:'|cut -d':' -f2| tr -d ' \t'`"
        rval=$?;;
"clients")
    value="`squidclient mgr:info|grep 'Number of clients accessing
cache:'|cut -d':' -f2| tr -d ' \t'`"
```

```
        rval=$?;;
"icp_received")
        value="`squidclient mgr:info|grep 'Number of ICP messages
received:'|cut -d':' -f2| tr -d ' \t'`"
        rval=$?;;
"icp_sent")
        value="`squidclient mgr:info|grep 'Number of ICP messages
sent:'|cut -d':' -f2| tr -d ' \t'`"
        rval=$?;;
"icp_queued")
        value="`squidclient mgr:info|grep 'Number of queued ICP
replies:'|cut -d':' -f2| tr -d ' \t'`"
        rval=$?;;
"htcp_received")
        value="`squidclient mgr:info|grep 'Number of HTCP messages
received:'|cut -d':' -f2| tr -d ' \t'`"
        rval=$?;;
"htcp_sent")
        value="`squidclient mgr:info|grep 'Number of HTCP messages
sent:'|cut -d':' -f2| tr -d ' \t'`"
        rval=$?;;
"req_fail_ratio")
        value="`squidclient mgr:info|grep 'Request failure ratio:'|cut
-d':' -f2| tr -d ' \t'`"
        rval=$?;;
"avg_http_req_per_min")
        value="`squidclient mgr:info|grep 'Average HTTP requests per
minute since start:'|cut -d':' -f2| tr -d ' \t'`"
        rval=$?;;
"avg_icp_msg_per_min")
        value="`squidclient mgr:info|grep 'Average ICP messages per
minute since start:'|cut -d':' -f2| tr -d ' \t'`"
        rval=$?;;
"request_hit_ratio")
        value="`squidclient mgr:info|grep 'Request Hit Ratios:'|cut
-d':' -f3|cut -d',' -f1|tr -d ' %'`"
        rval=$?;;
"byte_hit_ratio_5")
        value="`squidclient mgr:info|grep 'Hits as % of bytes sent:'|
awk -F'[:,% ]' '{print $10}'| tr -d ' \t'`"
        rval=$?;;
"byte_hit_ratio_60")
        value="`squidclient mgr:info|grep 'Hits as % of bytes sent:'|
awk -F'[:,% ]' '{print $15}'| tr -d ' \t'`"
        rval=$?;;
```

```
"request_mem_hit_ratio_5")
        value="`squidclient mgr:info|grep 'Hits as % of all requests:'
|  awk -F'[:,% ]' '{print $10}'| tr -d ' \t'`"
        rval=$?;;
"request_mem_hit_ratio_60")
        value="`squidclient mgr:info|grep 'Hits as % of all requests:'
|  awk -F'[:,% ]' '{print $15}'| tr -d ' \t'`"
        rval=$?;;
"request_disk_hit_ratio_5")
        value="`squidclient mgr:info|grep 'Disk hits as % of hit
requests:'|awk -F'[:,% ]' '{print $11}'| tr -d ' \t'`"
        rval=$?;;
"request_disk_hit_ratio_60")
        value="`squidclient mgr:info|grep 'Disk hits as % of hit
requests:'|awk -F'[:,% ]' '{print $16}'| tr -d ' \t'`"
        rval=$?;;
"servicetime_httpreq")
        value="`squidclient mgr:info|grep 'HTTP Requests (All):'|cut
-d':' -f2|tr -s ' '|awk '{print $1}'`"
        rval=$?;;
"process_mem")
        value="`squidclient mgr:info|grep 'Process Data Segment Size
via sbrk'|cut -d':' -f2|awk '{print $1}'`"
        rval=$?;;
"cpu_usage")
        value="`squidclient mgr:info|grep 'CPU Usage:'|cut -d':'
-f2|tr -d '%'|tr -d ' \t'`"
        rval=$?;;
"cache_size_disk")
        value="`squidclient mgr:info|grep 'Storage Swap size:'|cut
-d':' -f2|awk '{print $1}'`"
        rval=$?;;
"cache_size_mem")
        value="`squidclient mgr:info|grep 'Storage Mem size:'|cut
-d':' -f2|awk '{print $1}'`"
        rval=$?;;
"mean_obj_size")
        value="`squidclient mgr:info|grep 'Mean Object Size:'|cut
-d':' -f2|awk '{print $1}'`"
        rval=$?;;
"filedescr_max")
        value="`squidclient mgr:info|grep 'Maximum number of file
descriptors:'|cut -d':' -f2|awk '{print $1}'`"
        rval=$?;;
"filedescr_avail")
```

```
        value="`squidclient mgr:info|grep 'Available number of file
descriptors:'|cut -d':' -f2|awk '{print $1}'`"
        rval=$?;;
*)
        usage
        exit 1;;
esac

if [ "$rval" -eq 0 -a -z "$value" ]; then
        rval=1
fi

if [ "$rval" -ne 0 ]; then
        echo "ZBX_NOTSUPPORTED"
fi

echo $value
```

# Index

## Q

query_apachestats.py 85

## R

ReqPerSec parameter 87
rollstate plugin 78

## S

screen
  about 139
  creating 139
  graph, putting on 139
  maps, putting on 139
Siege
  URL 87
simple checks
  about 36
  configuring 38
  Icmpping 36
  Icmppingloss 36
  Icmppingsec 36
  Net.tcp.service 36
  Net.tcp.service.perf 36
slide show
  creating 142
SNMP (Simple Network Monitoring
      Protocol)
  about 39
  data, getting into Zabbix 40-43
  data types 53-57
  log file, monitoring with Zabbix 67, 68
  netflow data, receiving on server 63-66
  OIDs, finding for monitoring 43-47
  OIDs, mapping to Zabbix items 48-53
snmptrapd 58, 59
SNMP traps
  about 39, 57
  netflow, getting from devices 61-63
  snmptrapd 58, 59
  transforming, into Zabbix item 59-61
Squid
  about 93
  URL 93

Squid metric script 153
Squid monitoring
  performing 93-95
StartProxyPollers= parameter 15

## T

TCP/IP connection checks 36
trigger information cell 141
trigger overview cell 141

## V

value maps 54

## W

WaitingForConnection parameter 86
WebGUI interface
  installing 27-29

## X

xdot.py
  URL 128
xml2 72

## Z

Zabbix
  architectures 10, 11
  database, installing 20, 21
  data flow 12
  host groups 32
  hosts 32
  installing 16
  low-level discovery 98
  network discovery 98
  proxies data flow 13-16
Zabbix agent package, for Linux OS
  URL 19
Zabbix agents
  about 36
  simple checks 36-38
  SNMP 39
  SNMP traps 57

## Thank you for buying
# Zabbix Network Monitoring Essentials

## About Packt Publishing

Packt, pronounced 'packed', published its first book, *Mastering phpMyAdmin for Effective MySQL Management*, in April 2004, and subsequently continued to specialize in publishing highly focused books on specific technologies and solutions.

Our books and publications share the experiences of your fellow IT professionals in adapting and customizing today's systems, applications, and frameworks. Our solution-based books give you the knowledge and power to customize the software and technologies you're using to get the job done. Packt books are more specific and less general than the IT books you have seen in the past. Our unique business model allows us to bring you more focused information, giving you more of what you need to know, and less of what you don't.

Packt is a modern yet unique publishing company that focuses on producing quality, cutting-edge books for communities of developers, administrators, and newbies alike. For more information, please visit our website at www.packtpub.com.

## About Packt Open Source

In 2010, Packt launched two new brands, Packt Open Source and Packt Enterprise, in order to continue its focus on specialization. This book is part of the Packt Open Source brand, home to books published on software built around open source licenses, and offering information to anybody from advanced developers to budding web designers. The Open Source brand also runs Packt's Open Source Royalty Scheme, by which Packt gives a royalty to each open source project about whose software a book is sold.

## Writing for Packt

We welcome all inquiries from people who are interested in authoring. Book proposals should be sent to author@packtpub.com. If your book idea is still at an early stage and you would like to discuss it first before writing a formal book proposal, then please contact us; one of our commissioning editors will get in touch with you.

We're not just looking for published authors; if you have strong technical skills but no writing experience, our experienced editors can help you develop a writing career, or simply get some additional reward for your expertise.

## Mastering Zabbix

ISBN: 978-1-78328-349-1          Paperback: 358 pages

Monitor your large IT environment efficiently with Zabbix

1. Create the perfect monitoring configuration based on your specific needs.

2. Extract reports and visualizations from your data.

3. Integrate monitoring data with other systems in your environment.

4. Learn the advanced techniques of Zabbix to monitor networks and performances in large environments.

## Zabbix 1.8 Network Monitoring

ISBN: 978-1-84719-768-9          Paperback: 428 pages

Monitor your network's hardware, servers, and web performance effectively and efficiently

1. Start with the very basics of Zabbix, an enterprise-class open source network monitoring solution, and move up to more advanced tasks later.

2. Efficiently manage your hosts, users, and permissions.

3. Get alerts and react to changes in monitored parameters by sending out e-mails, SMSs, or even execute commands on remote machines.

## Zabbix Network Monitoring Essentials [Video]

ISBN: 978-1-78216-550-7          Duration: 02:33 hrs

Leverage the advanced features of Zabbix to set up a professional network monitoring system quickly and efficiently

1. Get a fast-paced tour through the essential parts of Zabbix.

2. Set up your own monitoring system so Zabbix can inform you if your IT infrastructure starts misbehaving.

3. Learn to make practical use of features you won't find in the documentation.

## Icinga Network Monitoring

ISBN: 978-1-78328-229-6          Paperback: 118 pages

Monitor complex and large environments across dispersed locations with Icinga

1. Installation instructions with detailed steps and explanations of configuration for complex networks with diagrams.

2. Extend Icinga with your own plugins and add-ons.

3. Sample configuration to give a clear understanding.

Please check **www.PacktPub.com** for information on our titles